Tall Tails and True Stories from Brown County

Larry Bullard

authorHOUSE

AuthorHouse™
1663 Liberty Drive
Bloomington, IN 47403
www.authorhouse.com
Phone: 1-800-839-8640

© 2010 Larry Bullard. All rights reserved.

No part of this book may be reproduced, stored in a retrieval system, or transmitted by any means without the written permission of the author.

First published by AuthorHouse 7/29/2010

ISBN: 978-1-4520-4159-9 (e)
ISBN: 978-1-4520-4160-5 (sc)
ISBN: 978-1-4520-4161-2 (hc)

Library of Congress Control Number: 2010909260

Printed in the United States of America
Bloomington, Indiana

This book is printed on acid-free paper.

Acknowledgments

This amusing little volume of tales charms the soul and brings a chuckle or two to refresh a tired mind. If you are burdened by the work you must do to put bread on the table, or have the concerns we all should have about the economy or strife in far off lands, just read several of Larry Bullard's stories and be transported back to a simpler life in Brown County, Illinois as it existed thirty years ago. To read these stories is to know a time when morality and wholesomeness were the stock in trade of family life.

                        David K. Slocum
                        Circuit Judge, Retired,
                        and local historian

"Tall Tails" will bring a smile to your face. Anyone who grew up on a farm will enjoy this book. Thanks for the memories, Larry!

                        Char Stocker
                        Great Debate Books,
                        Owner

While reading Larry's collection of stories, it brought back memories of growing up on the farm and all the fun my friends and I had making our own entertainment. We all look back and wish we had written down some of those crazy events or could better remember the details of what it was like as a kid. Larry does a wonderful job of reliving our childhood for us...what it was like for so many growing up in that era. But probably more important, he captures in a humorous way, a life that our kids and grandkids (and anyone not living on the farm) can only hear about or in this case read about. Thanks Larry, for making me laugh, but the best part was hearing my son chuckle as he read about a life that did not include video games or iPods and was a lot more entertaining.

Dale Gadberry, Pastor

Dedication

I am dedicating this book to my parents, Fred and Mittie. Their hard work ethic and strong Christian faith were a positive influence on family and friends. Although my parents have been gone several years, I can still visualize Mom working with her flowers or showing grandchildren interesting crafts. I can also see Dad giving children rides in a small wagon pulled by a goat. Memories of Dad and Mom will always be special.

My wife was very instrumental in the completion of this book. Her encouragement, along with that of our children, Rachel, Shawn, and Andrew, helped transform the dream of writing a book into reality. Monte, thank you so much for changing my chicken-scratch design for the front cover into a work of art! I would also like to thank other important members of our team, Karie and Marilyn. Your help was sincerely appreciated.

Larry Bullard

Introduction

Several of the stories that you are about to read are based on actual occurrences. Some are 100% true and others are about as straight as a dog's hind leg. Most of the names have been changed to protect the innocent, or not so innocent.

Writing this book was a serious challenge for me. Cutting hedge posts would have been much simpler. Most of you will be able to tell by my use of the English language and my structure of sentences that I am definitely out of my comfort zone.

Hopefully, readers will be able to glimpse a somewhat typical life of a boy growing up on a small farm in Brown County, IL. Prior to the advent of many modern technologies, we children were encouraged to create our own entertainment. Some of those forms of entertainment may seem strange to a young person today. I, on the other hand, have difficulty understanding the concept of typing words on a cell phone or bowling in front of a TV on a Wii.

These stories are based on simple segments of my life, but I hope everyone will enjoy the trip as you travel with me through some interesting days of my past.

Table of Contents

Chapter 1	Skunked	1
Chapter 2	The Dremel Tool Kit	8
Chapter 3	Bottoms Up	13
Chapter 4	Entertainment	20
Chapter 5	The Bird Herd	23
Chapter 6	Berry Pickin'	29
Chapter 7	Pets	35
Chapter 8	Taj Mahal	41
Chapter 9	Buddies	46
Chapter 10	Knothead	57
Chapter 11	Hay, Hay, Hay	63
Chapter 12	The Hornet Nest	71
Chapter 13	A Promise Kept	81
Chapter 14	Stupid Is As Stupid Does	86
Chapter 15	Grunt	91
Chapter 16	Dreams or Nightmares?	97
Chapter 17	Sam	103
Chapter 18	Shoot Doggone	109
Chapter 19	Scat	117

Chapter 1

Skunked

It seems the older I get, the more questions I have about the simple things of life, and the more confused I become. I still haven't figured out which dress shirt to wear with the beige slacks or why I need to wear black socks instead of white ones.

Remember when we only had one knob to turn in order to watch TV? Now there are three remotes on our coffee table with fifty buttons on each one. My wife and I seldom watch a DVD because when we do, we usually have to call our daughter for technical assistance.

Life seems complicated enough without all these technologies. Farmers used to be able to work on their own tractor engines with just a few wrenches and a screwdriver. Now you can't begin to work on one without a diagnostic computer. I keep an old Oliver 66 around just so I can remember what the "good old days" were like.

I'm the type of person who would be content to eat a meal of meat, mashed potatoes and gravy, and a vegetable every day. Sometimes I cringe when my wife announces that we are having something different for supper. In all honesty, though, I haven't suffered from a case of food poisoning – yet.

Apples never fall far from the tree, so I blame my reluctance to try new things on Dad. Microwaves had been popular ten years before Dad brought one home for Mom's Christmas present. A diamond ring wouldn't have pleased her more. That night, Mom tried it for the first time and fixed Dad's favorite – pork chops. Mom cooked those pork chops, and cooked them, until they were the golden brown color that she was familiar with. When we sat down for supper, I wondered why a pair of tongs were lying on the plate of pork chops instead of the usual old fork. After Dad said a blessing for supper, Mom passed the platter of pork chops around the table. Dad was the first to try the delicious-looking chops. After failing to imbed his fork into the meat, he changed tactics and picked it up with his fingers. When he finally broke a piece off with his teeth, the rest of the pork chop shattered in his hand and fell around his plate. Dad took a long drink of water and then tried his best to compliment the cook.

"Well, it tastes good," he said, "but I can't tell where the bone stops and the meat starts!"

One might label me as being conservative until it comes to deer hunting. Deer hunting is my passion and I have tried my best to keep up with the latest technologies. I have camouflaged clothes now and a nice bow that even has a sight. After my last hunt, though, it will be many years before I try something new and improved. Maybe I should receive a gold medal for being a survivor of this

Skunked

adventure, but if the emblem on the medal corresponded with the actions involved, I would be too humiliated to wear it in public.

It was a warm November afternoon, and I had one of those sudden impulses to go bow hunting. There was plenty of work to do at home. Some of those were jobs my wife thought I had done two weeks ago, but I kept thinking about that huge buck I had seen several times grazing in our wheat field. I was also anxious to try a different method than hunting from my permanent wooden tree stand. A neighbor had shared with me his experience of harvesting a large buck while hunting from a camouflaged deer blind – one of those pop-up kind. He was so excited, he convinced me to buy one, also. This afternoon, although a little windy, would be a perfect time to try it out. Little did I know what surprises lay ahead.

By 2:30 that afternoon, all of my gear was ready. I had even practiced setting the blind up and taking it back down. As I hauled everything over to the wheat field in my truck, I was optimistic of my chances of shooting that big buck. I carried my bow, the camouflaged deer blind, my wife's favorite lawn chair, my camera, everything I would possibly need across the wheat field. Since I wouldn't be climbing down from a tree stand in the dark, it didn't seem necessary to carry my big flashlight, so I left it in the truck along with my common sense. Hind sight is always 20-20.

I set the blind up approximately twenty feet from a brush pile which was close to the wheat field. A westerly wind was blowing hard enough to require pushing two small tent stakes into the ground on the west side of the blind. Driving those two little tent stakes into the ground would prove to make my evening quite memorable.

After zipping the door shut, and opening the shooting windows, I made myself comfortable in the lawn chair. "Man, this is so much nicer than my old wooden tree stand," I thought. The ground blind didn't have a floor so while relaxing in the chair, I happened to notice that the chair was sitting directly over a small well-worn path which extended from the brush pile out into the wheat field. The path was probably made by many rabbits going back and forth. Wouldn't it be neat if a rabbit found its way into the blind? Taking wildlife pictures was one of my hobbies and this could be a good opportunity. I readied my camera and rested it on my right knee and laid my bow across both legs.

Right before dusk, several does and a spike buck came out of the wheat field, totally ignoring my deer blind, which probably looked to them like another brush pile. My neighbor was right. This worked better than expected. Finally, a beautiful 12-point buck stepped out of the woods just fifty yards away. I thought I could hear my heartbeat echo in the blind and my knees began to shake. I had never seen a buck this big! I'm sure that many of you have shared this thrill but this is where we draw the line. Few, if any, can relate to the next hour of my life.

As the buck took another step closer, I remembered the camera and knew I had to get it off my knee. As I looked down to move the camera, it was all I could do to suppress the urge to scream. A large skunk had crawled into the blind and was sniffing my boot with his tail at half-mast. Why oh why couldn't it have been a cute little rabbit?!

If any of you have a blind like the one that imprisoned me, now you have the advantage of knowing what can happen and can plan accordingly. I'm quite positive that the college graduate that designed these blinds didn't do the field testing himself. At the moment, I felt like a wolf with no teeth in a flock of sheep. What do I do now?!

If I could push the blind up off the ground using my bow, maybe the skunk would find his way out. When the skunk moved directly under my chair, I quietly tried to reach the top of the blind with my bow. Since my wife's chair was short, I couldn't reach the roof. In this position, I noticed that the huge buck was only twenty yards away from the window. The chance of a lifetime was right before me and I was frozen like a petrified log.

By now, I was in panic mode with sweat running down my face. I would have to stand up quickly, lift the blind, and then run, carrying the blind with me. That's when things went downhill. As I stood up, I forgot about the camera. It hit the ground with a click and a flash. To the skunk, this was probably comparable to lightning striking his brush pile. To make matters worse, remember those two little tent stakes? I didn't. I highly respect the individual who designed these simple, yet ingenious, anchors. They held one side of that blind down like steel posts. Instead of running away carrying the blind like a giant umbrella, I found myself falling backwards, collapsing the chair on a temporarily blinded and startled skunk. The blind then came down wrapping the skunk and I in absolute darkness.

You just had to be there to understand how much I wanted to be back in my favorite old tree stand. There were legs kicking, arms thrashing against a broken lawn chair, camouflaged walls being ripped and one enraged skunk doing his best to saturate what little air was left with the most effective self-defense weapon on earth. Maybe it was my screams that infuriated the skunk so badly. It began making hissing sounds. On second thought, it was probably just sucking more air in to assist the spraying mechanism on the other end.

After what seemed like three eternities, I managed to extricate myself from the tangle of bent arrows, torn up blind, lawn chair webbing, and a thick fog of skunk. I decided to leave all of my gear at the crime scene with the skunk. My eyes were burning so badly, tears were flowing. I couldn't tell if it was dark because it was dark or if I was completely blinded by the skunk's spray. As I staggered across the field toward my truck, sometimes on all fours, I wondered what county that big buck was in and if he would ever get close to another brush pile.

I finally found the truck and left another pile of evidence: all of my hunting clothes and boots. Using toilet paper (all well-prepared hunters carry a roll in their truck) to hold onto the steering wheel, and driving with the windows down, I made it home.

My wife happened to be by the garage ready to leave for choir practice when I pulled into the driveway. One can only imagine what thoughts went through her mind when

I ejected from the truck dressed only in my briefs and socks with sheets of toilet paper stuck to my hands!

"Why, honey, where are your clothes?" she asked. "Why are you crying? Oh, good Lord, what's that horrible smell?"

I wonder if sometime in another century a simpler version of this nightmare occurred, maybe in pioneer times, when another ill-fated hunter invented the two-word phrase that I would use to answer my wife's questions.

"Got skunked!"

CHAPTER 2

The Dremel Tool Kit

Reflecting about the advance of new technology reminds me of a neat Christmas gift I received several years ago. I love working with wood. For many years I cut hedge posts and firewood to sell for additional income. It was very hard work, but that isn't the enjoyable type of woodworking I am referring to.

About fifteen years ago, I became interested in rustic furniture and began making willow chairs. Eventually, I branched out into other areas, making tables and benches. Building rustic furniture doesn't require expensive woodworking machines or the exactness of making more modern furniture. Both of these factors suited me just fine. I could utilize small, inexpensive tools and if I goofed up, which I still do in making primitive furniture, no one would notice.

My daughter, Rachel, and her husband, Danny, surprised me this particular Christmas with a Dremel Tool Kit. For those of you who aren't carpenters, a Dremel Tool is a multi-purpose variable speed tool. It is similar to a hand-held drill but much smaller with several different attachments available and a much greater capacity for high speeds. I was anxious to use it for engraving.

The first Sunday afternoon following Christmas, Danny and Rachel stopped by to visit. Danny, who is an avid basketball fan, was proudly wearing a present he had received from Rachel. It was a great looking white sweatshirt with Chicago Bulls in bold lettering on the back. On the front in bold colors was the face of a red bull. I'm sure he still has this sweatshirt, but he hasn't been brave enough to wear it to our house since that day.

Rachel asked if I had tried engraving with the Dremel Tool yet. I hadn't taken the time to work with it but thought, why not now? All three of us could experiment with it.

It was much too cold to be comfortable in my workshop, so I brought in a small cedar board and set it on our island bar in the kitchen. I placed a small engraving bit onto the business-end of the Dremel Tool and plugged it into an electrical outlet. I began by trying to etch the shape of a deer into the board but my progress was very limited. Even though the Dremel was smaller than a cordless drill, it still felt too bulky and awkward in my clumsy hand. But alas! The engineers who manufactured the Dremel were way ahead of me! Included in the tool kit was a forty-inch flexible shaft. You simply attach one end of the shaft to the Dremel and place whatever bit you want on the other end of the shaft. Holding the working end of the flex shaft would be similar to holding a fat pencil and would be much easier to manipulate. The operator's manual was very explicit about hazards associated with the tool. CAUTION, CAUTION, CAUTION, in bold letters:

When using the flex shaft, insure that the Dremel Tool is hung from a very stationary object before using!!! I attached the flex shaft to the Dremel and inserted a bit into the other end of the shaft. Now we were ready for business.

All three of us were sitting on bar stools around our kitchen island. I was on the right side, Danny was on my left and Rachel was around the corner of the island on Danny's left. All three of us looked around trying to find a stationary object that was located in a convenient place which would allow us to use the island as a work area. We drew a complete blank. Rachel and I looked at each other and I think we came up with a solution at the same time. Remember, apples never fall far from the tree. Danny, being the newest addition to our family, was unanimously volunteered to become the stationary object. After all, Danny has always been an exceptional athlete and is as solid as a brick outhouse, and he was sitting in the middle.

I handed the Dremel Tool to Danny. On the back end of the tool was a small metal ring for hanging it up, so Danny placed a finger through the ring and lifted his hand high in the air. I stood up and adjusted the speed on the Dremel Tool to the highest setting, which was 30,000 rpm.

Just try to visualize the picture: Danny was sitting between Rachel and I with his right hand high in the air, a high-speed motor hanging from his index finger, and a greenhorn was holding the vibrating flex shaft that was humming like a dentist drill on steroids.

As I began engraving the board, little wisps of cedar smoke started rising from my artwork. I was surprised how much easier it was using the flex shaft. Rachel wanted to experiment, also. I was afraid Danny's arm would be getting tired so instead of wasting time in turning off the machine, I just slid the cedar board toward Rachel and tried to hand her the flex shaft. Holding that flex shaft on full speed would be similar to picking up a miniature fire hose and suddenly having the pressure turned up to the max. As I released my grip on the shaft, Rachel panicked and let go, also. What happened next was simply amazing! The high-speed black snake with a sharp bit in its mouth whipped a large circle in the air and then attacked that red bull right in the nose. Instantly, the front of Danny's sweatshirt was twisted up resembling a small pile of rope.

Tears were rolling down my cheeks, but I was too tickled to laugh out loud. My chest hurt and I thought I was going to need a paper bag to breathe into. Rachel laughed so hard, she slid off her bar stool and made a <u>futile</u> attempt to reach the bathroom before having an accident.

Danny looked like he was in shock. His face was as white as his sweatshirt. His new sweatshirt was twisted up so tight that his shoulders hunched forward. I unplugged the Dremel cord and began to unwind Danny from the snake. I expected the red bull to have a real hole for a nostril instead of a fake one. It still amazes me that his sweatshirt wasn't damaged in any way.

Danny passed his initiation into our unusual family exploits without any injuries. Today, Danny is much more cautious when Rachel and I put our heads together. I can't understand why.

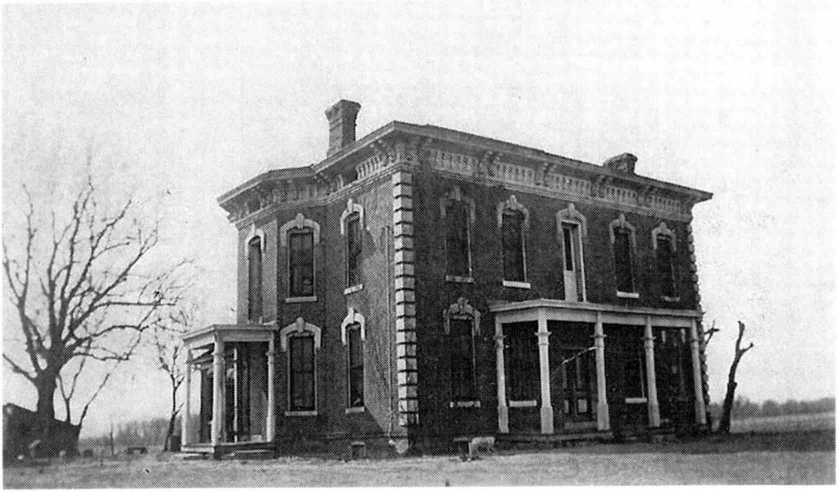

CHAPTER 3

Bottoms Up

The brick house where our family lived wasn't the typical farmhouse for Brown County. In its day, it would have been considered a mansion, but its day was around 1900. Captain Sylvester Nokes began construction on the house in 1881. The bricks were made from clay that was dug by hand on the farm. The clay was placed into molds that were placed in the sun to dry. There is a date of October 1882 etched into a brick near the eaves of the roof. The farm was originally an apple orchard. Crates of apples were stored in the cool, damp basement and hives of honey bees were kept in the third story, which consisted of one large room. Holes had been drilled in the window frames to allow the bees passage to and from the hives.

At the time we were living in the house, bees were no longer present, but three or four empty hives stilled remained. Bats were a nuisance as they would crawl in under the eaves of the roof and roost in the nooks and crannies of the rafters. Sometimes, my sisters or my cousins and I would go up to the third story in the daytime with badminton racquets. One of us would intentionally irritate the bats until they began flying around the room. We would then play "bat-minton." You had to be careful not to hit each other with the racquets. We actually swatted more air than bats as they were very adept at dodging our swings.

There were seven large bedrooms, a large living room and dining room, a big kitchen, but only one small bathroom. The ceilings were ten feet high and each doorway had a transom window above the door. Opening these windows helped ventilate the house during the hot summer days.

The house was originally heated by three large fireplaces. When our family lived there, the house was heated by an old coal furnace which was in the basement. Coal was scooped into a small bin, or stoker, and then an internal auger would move the coal into the furnace. At night you could hear a loud grinding noise as the auger did its job. Overnight guests had to be reassured that they weren't hearing ghosts. One of my daily jobs during the cold season was to keep the stoker full of coal and also to remove the clinkers from the furnace. We would carry buckets of clinkers out to the hog lot. It sent chills up my back to hear our old sows chomping on those clinkers. It sounded like their teeth were breaking.

In the living room, there was one register in the ceiling which was the only source of heat for the four bedrooms on the second floor. One winter I decided to sleep upstairs for more privacy. It was so cold you couldn't leave any liquid sitting out because it would freeze.

I will never forget climbing the stairs one day headed toward my bedroom while eating a banana. At the top of the stairs, a bat suddenly flew into the banana I was holding in my hand. I'm not sure which one of us was more surprised.

On the main stairway was a very ornate curved banister that we loved to slide down. Maybe the builder foresaw this happening because the post at the bottom had a large flattened out area on top of it. The handrail was slick from years of rump-polishing so sometimes first-timers ended up with a painful experience if they didn't hold on tight!

In the third story room there was a ladder going up to the roof. There was a flat area approximately 8-feet by 10 feet where you could stand and have a wonderful view of the surrounding area. One winter, Dad built a large wooden cross with several lights on it and erected it on the flat roof for the Christmas season. At night it was visible for several miles.

My two sisters and I have many fond memories of growing up in the old brick house. Some of the memories are painful but the humorous ones are much easier to remember. Linda, Karis, and I believe that if we can't laugh at ourselves, we shouldn't laugh at each other. We do both quite often. Linda has probably forgotten about an incident that I will share with you. I feel it is important for her family to know her dark secret. You can thank me later, Sis.

Although we did have a small bathroom, we still utilized an outhouse out by the chicken yard. When Linda started high school, her visits to the outhouse became less frequent. It was unbecoming for a lady of her age to degrade herself to such levels. One night Linda ran into the house, apparently waiting until the last moment to use the bathroom. To her dismay, Karis was already in the bathroom, so Linda begrudgingly grabbed a flashlight and headed for the outhouse. I thought it was funny that as soon as Linda walked outside, Karis came out of the bathroom. Terrible screams were heard outside. The screaming Linda rushed into the house, ran into the bathroom, and slammed the door. She kept screaming and sobbing until Mom went in to see what was wrong. Linda finally came out with a towel wrapped around her and she was carrying her wadded-up pair of peddle-pushers. After Linda disappeared, Mom told us what happened to Sis. Linda was barefoot as she walked down the path to the outhouse and stepped on a large snake which curled around her foot. Needless to say, she didn't need to finish her journey!

Dad was a humble man, but I think he was somewhat proud of our brick outhouse. It was unusual in the fact that it was a 3-holer. The seat was just a very wide board with three round holes in it. I still haven't figured out why it had three holes in it. I could understand the small hole for small bottoms and the large hole for larger bottoms, but why it had two large holes, I'll never know. It really wasn't the best atmosphere to socialize in. We never witnessed two people using it at the same time, let alone three.

When it was cold and sitting down was required, you quickly learned to sit toward the front of the hole to reduce the amount of bare bottom that touched the cold wood. When it wasn't cold, you waited until the very last moment to use the facility because of the aroma and there was always the chance of getting stung by bumble bees that frequented the outhouse.

Whoever built the outhouse must have had long-legged children. I had to stand on two bricks to get into position over the small hole. My older sisters had graduated to the large holes, or I assumed they did. It wasn't a subject they cared to discuss. I could hardly wait to move over and sit on one of the large holes. To me, it was as important as growing enough to be able to drive Dad's tractor. Dad never told me when I could try the big hole. It was one of those things you had to learn on your own.

Dad had very poor eyesight when I was young. One spring, neighbors even planted his crops for him as he was nearly blind. Dad and I missed some of the things fathers and sons do, like playing ball or hunting together, but the bond we shared was very strong. Although not very big, I helped Dad as much as I could, especially in taking care of the livestock. Sometimes we would use a tractor to haul a wagon load of hay to the cows or corn to the hogs. Our method was unusual but it worked for us. Dad couldn't see well enough to drive the tractor so I would sit on his lap and be his eyes for him. When we got close to a gate, I would tell him to stop. We would get off the tractor and I would lead him to the gate. After we got the gate open, I would lead him back to the tractor.

Over a period of two or three years, Dad underwent seven or eight surgeries and wore patches over one eye or sometimes both eyes. I am sure doctors today wouldn't have allowed him to do any physical activity with such serious eye problems. To Dad, though, his faith and his hard work ethics were the very essence of life. He continued to work hard and refused to give in to his vision impairment.

One day, Dad gave me a rare pat on the back for completing a task he would normally have to do. "You're growing up fast, son," he said. I grew two bricks taller that day. Walking through the muddy lot with my hand in Dad's, I knew I was big enough to move over to that big hole. I could hardly wait for Mother Nature to call for #2.

The important time of my life had finally arrived. None of my family or friends would share the proud moment of my life. There wouldn't be any applause when I came out of the outhouse. All of that didn't matter. I just knew I would be a different person. I stepped in and latched the door from the inside. I didn't want anyone to barge in on my moment of glory. The two bricks were pushed over into the corner, never to be used again. I was a man now. I unbuckled my belt, pulled down my jeans and drawers and backed up to the seat. I knew I would have to jump up a little bit, but that didn't bother me. I put my hands on the edge of the seat and jumped up and backwards, landing right <u>IN</u> the large hole up to my armpits and knees! The only thing that kept me from disappearing into the darkness below was locking my hands onto the edges of the holes on either side of me. There I sat, or more appropriately, there I hung! I can't describe how deflated I was.

A bumble bee started flying around somewhere above my head sounding like an Apache helicopter. It was hot hanging there and the evidence of previous occupants was becoming more noticeable. I had to get myself out of this alone. My manhood was at stake!

With my knees almost touching my nose, it was easy to notice my belt. I pulled sideways as much as I dared with my left arm and released the death-grip of my right hand. I was able to wriggle the belt out of the belt loops on my jeans. Thank goodness I decided not to wear my bib-overalls that day! There was a big nail on the wall above my head where we hung the flyswatter. The nail was low enough that I was able to reach up and put my belt buckle over it. By now, my legs were numb. As I pulled up on the belt, I wriggled my rear end and the large hole finally released its bare-bottomed captive. My legs were tingling all over regaining circulation. I was sure relieved in more ways than one. Someday, I hoped my bottom would be bigger.

At the supper table that night, I looked into my sisters' faces and wondered if it was as difficult for them to become women as it was for me to become a man.

CHAPTER 4

Entertainment

It saddens me in this modern era as I watch children spend hours and hours each day in front of the TV or playing video games. I feel fortunate that I grew up playing outside most of the time. Yes, we did have TV but we only watched it when we weren't visiting with neighbors or when the weather confined us inside. As children, we weren't allowed to watch tv during the day. Karis and I would play some board games together but usually I would create my own entertainment.

One of my favorite indoor past-times was removing the bottom from a Quaker oats container and taping it to the back of the door that went from our dining room into the living room. I would then move some of the furniture out of the way and have a small area to play basketball with a small rubber ball or ping pong ball. I never lost because I never had any competition. Karis wasn't into professional basketball.

Outdoors, we enjoyed playing "hand-me-over" using a rubber ball that is thrown over the garage roof. I also enjoyed throwing rocks or looking for fossils in our gravel lane or down in the creek.

I'm sure that today there is a higher than normal amount of copper on the farm where we lived. Most of my chore money was used to buy BB's and .22 rifle shells. I don't remember breaking any windows with my BB gun but I sure put a lot of dents in the side of the barn.

There were large vines on one side of our brick house and sparrows continually built nests in the vines. Occasionally, I would lay on my back in the yard, halfway between the house and a large maple tree. I would then shoot at sparrows in the air as they flew directly over me. Once, I hit a large blackbird. The BB didn't knock him out of the air but it did knock something out of the bird. SPLAT – right on my face!

There was a large cupola on top of the barn. On top of the cupola was a weathervane with a horse on one end of the arrow. Sometimes when I knew Dad wasn't around, I would try to shoot the horse. A few years before Dad passed away, we removed the weathervane from the roof of the barn. Dad's eyesight was very poor so he was surprised to see such a "holey" horse. My brother and I couldn't convince him that hail had done the damage, especially since there were dents on the bottom of the horse's hooves. We sheepishly admitted it was due to our superb marksmanship. Dad wasn't very angry. He shared with us that when he was young, he spotted a hornet nest in a tree about 50 yards from where he and his dad were standing. Dad wanted to shoot at it with his rifle but Granddad told him not to. Later that day, Dad went back to the same place and shot at the nest. He said

Tall Tails and True Stories from Brown County

as soon as he shot, a hornet nailed him right between the eyes. He thought he had been shot!

Today that weathervane with the patched-up holey horse sits on my garage roof. Each time I look at it, wonderful memories return.

Chapter 5

The Bird Herd

"These eggs aren't nearly as good as farm-grown eggs," I complained at the breakfast table to my wife.

Cindy agreed and then helped initiate another interesting chapter in my life by stating,

"Well, why don't you quit complaining about it and raise your own chickens?"

At first, I was opposed to her idea. Hard-headed husbands tend to appreciate their wives' ideas much less than their own.

My next breakfast of pale, flat-tasting store-bought eggs encouraged me to seriously consider her idea. We did have an old shed that could be repaired enough to accommodate some chickens, and I could bury an electric wire from our garage to the shed to provide lighting.

The thought of our grandchildren also played an important role in my decision to purchase some chickens. When our children were young, part of their responsibilities was to help care for the livestock we had.

Although they weren't old enough to milk Bambi, our Jersey milk cow, they did help feed her, also the sheep and chickens. Our kids still remember having to take turns at the butter churn. I think their favorite chore was to gather the eggs. I felt like our grandchildren would appreciate coming to Grammy and Papa's farm to see cute little chickens and help gather eggs.

The old shed that was to be our chicken house had been used as a hog house for many years and hadn't been cleaned out. It took several hours of scooping and breathing hog dust and dried manure to get the shed clean. I then built a large outdoor enclosure (chicken yard) adjoining the shed and ran the electric wire for lighting.

Our neighbor had given me a poultry catalog which had pictures of many kinds of domestic and exotic breeds of chickens. When I was young, Mom always had white Leghorns and a few small Bantams – or what we called Banties. I decided it would be more interesting for our grandchildren if we had an assortment of breeds and colors in our herd of birds.

I ordered 30 day-old chicks from about 7 different breeds, which included some small Banties. When they arrived a few days later, we placed them in a heated area in the chicken house. The next evening, our granddaughters saw the little chicks for the first time and fell in love with them. It was a neat experience for them to hold the cute fuzzy chicks in their hands, but it was much more special for Grammy and Papa to watch.

Two weeks later, our granddaughters were back, but to their dismay the cute little chicks had changed. The chicks' feathers had started to grow and they were at that scraggly-looking stage. Although the girls would pet the chicks, the desire to hold them in their hands was gone.

As the chicks matured into chickens, it was interesting to see the variation of colors and notice the different personalities. There were five roosters, two of which were Banties. Of the other three, one red rooster was much larger than the other two.

One of the hens was a Polish breed. It had a large top-knot on its head resembling a helmet. The feathers hung down over its eyes blocking its forward vision completely. It would walk in to obstructions and finally learned to walk sideways to avoid bumping into things.

Summertime was upon us and I began releasing the chickens from the chicken yard in the daytime hours. Their range included our yard and the garden area. They were constantly chasing grasshoppers and crickets and eventually, two little girls.

For some unknown reason, what Banties lack in stature, they make up for it in aggressiveness. One day, our oldest granddaughter, Kylie, who was only six at the time, was playing with our cat out in the yard. Her frantic screams were heard where I was working in the garden. When I got to her, she was standing still, too scared to run. A Banty rooster was standing near her with his wings outspread and the feathers on his back raised up. A boot-induced launch of a tail-feathered chicken butt rescued Kylie, but from that day on, chickens were removed from Kylie's list of favorite animals.

The following week I rediscovered the relevance of the

phrase, "You're just a big chicken." One day after lunch, I was sitting on the bottom step of our deck putting on my work shoes. Several chickens were in the yard searching for bugs. Our large red rooster was among them acting like he was the "head honcho" until a little Banty rooster emerged from behind our magnolia tree. I think Mr. Banty must have been listening to Big Red crowing about himself and just couldn't take it anymore. The little Banty lowered his head and made a beeline for Big Red. The race was on! They made several circles around the driveway and then headed in my direction. It was hilarious to watch! When Big Red ran within three feet from where I was sitting, the word just blurted out, "CHICKEN!" Sometimes, I really surprise myself with what comes out of my mouth.

We had the chickens for three years and even became attached to them. Of course, the delicious eggs helped in that regard. When fall arrived that third year, two of our chickens disappeared. I didn't let the chickens out of their enclosure after that. A few mornings later, I found a dead chicken in the chicken house and coon tracks in the dust. That's all I needed – the war was on!

That night about midnight, I quietly left our house and crept around the garage with my shotgun and flashlight. I nailed two of the enemy as they were trying to scratch their way into the chicken house. That process became a nightly routine for me. The enemy kept returning and I kept dwindling their numbers.

The chickens stopped laying completely because of the battle going on around them.

After two weeks, the coon warfare was taking its

The Bird Herd

toll on me. We had lost three more chickens and I was becoming tired of getting dressed in the middle of the night, putting on my work shoes and sneaking around like G.I. Joe.

One exceptionally warm night, I couldn't sleep very well. At 2:00 a.m., I slipped out of the house clad only in my briefs and a pair of flip flops carrying my shotgun and flashlight. I worked my way around the garage toward the chicken house. Two large raccoons ran from the chicken house in the direction of the blacktop road which parallels our property. I was able to dispatch one of the varmints but the other one ran across the road before I could put another shell into my gun. Normally, I would have given up and gone back to bed, but that night, I wasn't taking any prisoners and wasn't letting any escape.

I crossed the road and could still see the raccoon in the beam of my flashlight as it ran toward some trees one-half mile away. Have you ever tried to run across a field of soybean stubble in a pair of flipflops? If my neighbors had witnessed my adventure, they would have called into the Sheriff's office to report an unidentified light beam. I stumbled several times. My light beam probably looked like a tug-boat searchlight looking for a safe route on a crooked river.

Finally, before I was completely out of breath, I was able to catch up to the raccoon and end the night's battle. As I shot the critter, I clumsily dropped my flashlight which quit working. "Shoot, doggone!" It was then that the realization of where I was and what I was doing struck home! Please believe me, standing out in the middle of an 80 acre bean field at 2:30 A.M. dressed only in briefs and flipflops and holding a shotgun is not normal for anyone, even me!

As I started my long awkward trek back toward home, headlights appeared approximately one mile away and were headed in the direction of our house. I sure hoped my wife hadn't awakened, found me missing, and called for a search party. My mind was racing trying to come up with a reason if someone stopped me to ask what in the world I was doing. The only conclusion I could come up with was to say I was just sleep-walking again. Thank goodness the car never stopped and my wife was still sound asleep when I climbed back into bed.

Shortly after my night out, we gave our remaining chickens to a neighbor who also wasn't happy with store-bought eggs.

Being a little wiser now, I've learned not to complain at breakfast and quietly eat my bowl of oatmeal.

Chapter 6

Berry Pickin'

It must have been 95 degrees. Sweat was running down my forehead and into my eyes, but I felt like I was in hog heaven. I was standing in the middle of a large patch of wild black raspberries. These little berries made the best jelly imaginable. My wife still makes a big batch every year that we share with family and friends.

Blackberries are more common in our neck of the woods and a lot easier to pick. The briars aren't as long as the raspberry briars and the berries are twice as big. One summer, with our kids helping, we sold enough blackberries to finance a mini vacation. The kids weren't too eager to help but they chose the berry patch over pulling weeds out of our bean field. Farming technology has advanced so much in the last few years that hardly anyone gets to enjoy walking beans.

Raspberries tend to grow in hard-to-get places. The patch I was in had grown over several piles of brush and dirt that a bull dozer had left years ago. The footing was very unsteady and several times I found myself balancing on broken branches. Raspberries are more tedious to pick and the briars so long, you can become entangled before you realize it with thorns digging into your clothes and skin. As a kid, I remember watching Mom and Dad picking berries wearing long-sleeved shirts and continually being snagged by the briars. Even then I enjoyed picking berries, but over the years I adapted a more unconventional method. When I find a patch of berries that looks promising, the first thing I do is throw a large stick, hedge apple, or rock into the middle of the patch. A few berries may be lost in this procedure, but it helps put my mind at ease. You just never know what might be lurking in the tangle of briars.

I remember one time having the be-gee-bees scared out of me when a turkey flew up right in front of my face. My greater concern involved a much more formidable adversary. Skunks like the shady environment of briar patches and brush piles. Just the word "skunk" sends chills up my back and makes my eyes water. The next thing I do is get topless. Yes, you read it right....topless. OK, so you agree with my wife that I am half a bubble off from being level. After getting topless, I unbuckle my belt. No, I'm not getting naked, remember, I'm just <u>half</u> a bubble off. I thread my belt through the handle of a 3-gallon bucket and then buckle up. Now the bucket hangs directly in front of me. Even my wife agrees I can pick berries much faster this way, using both hands. No amount of persuasion, however, could convince her to adopt my technique.

Berry Pickin'

    Picking berries using my method can be painful at times. Sometimes after filling my bucket, I look like I lost a fight with a cat, but I still prefer the scratches over the aggravation of having to untangle briars from shirt sleeves. Another advantage is that those pesky little wood ticks show up much better on bare skin. I'm sure there is a reason why God created these critters, but as of yet, He hasn't shared that information with me.

    OUCH! Raspberries should be worth $10.00 a pint, I thought, as I pulled a sticker from my arm. Just a few more handfuls and my bucket would be full. I started thinking about that jug of ice water in my pickup when I felt something hard, like a stick, push against my ankle inside my pant leg. I moved my left foot backwards slightly on the uneven ground but whatever was against my ankle didn't fall away. Instead, it started inching its way up my leg! I raised my left foot and stomped it on the ground hoping to dislodge whatever it was that was causing my blood pressure to soar. It didn't work! The unknown assailant continued to climb. I began slapping my leg with one hand while trying to unbuckle my belt and jeans with the other. By the time it reached the crotch of my jeans, the full bucket of berries had been sent into orbit. Even the yells didn't seem to affect the monster inside my jeans. Just try to picture this scene in your mind. The first thing you would notice would be a large white bucket flying through the air scattering raspberries through the air like a hail storm. Then the yells would draw your attention to what apparently was a deranged man with no shirt making all sorts of contortions and slapping himself on the lower half of his body.

From another viewpoint, you are an innocent little animal that decides to crawl up a tree that you have never explored before. On the way up, limbs from this strange tree try to grab at you from the darkness. Thinking some predator is in pursuit, you climb even higher. Then an enormous paw starts beating you on the back. You continue climbing higher until you hear loud roaring which must mean you are going the wrong way! Then you find another tree and climb down as fast as you can, continually being slapped by that giant paw. You are so scared you leave a yellow trail down the trunk marking the dangerous area, knowing you will never climb this weird tree again! Finally, you see daylight and safety.

Sometimes in life, it is a very good thing not to have a witness. Now was a perfect example. By now the creature was crawling down my other leg and I continued my strange dance and also kept beating my leg with both hands as the bucket of berries no longer hindered my movements. I sure didn't want the thing to change its path and start climbing back up again! My jeans buckle popped open so I pulled my jeans down to my knees. Finally a large lizard slid out of my right pant leg and slithered away into the briars. I remained bent over for a few minutes catching my breath and realized I had actually pulled some muscles in my back.

I enjoy watching any history shows associated with the numerous tribes of American Indians. Their culture is quite interesting. The traditional tribal dances are mesmerizing to me. Some of the dance moves are probably passed down from generation to generation. Outsiders don't have a clue what a lot of the high steps and arm waving relate to. I may have accidentally stumbled onto a hidden secret. Maybe their ancestors also endured the trials and tribulations of picking wild raspberries.

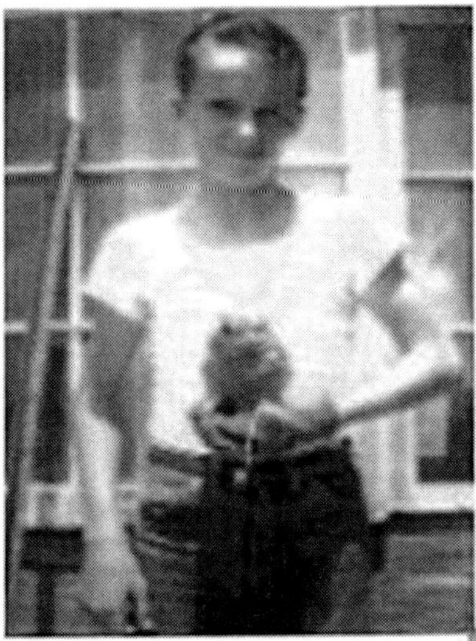

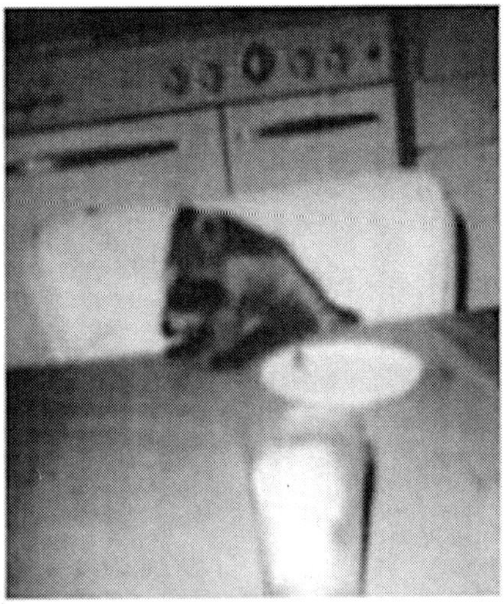

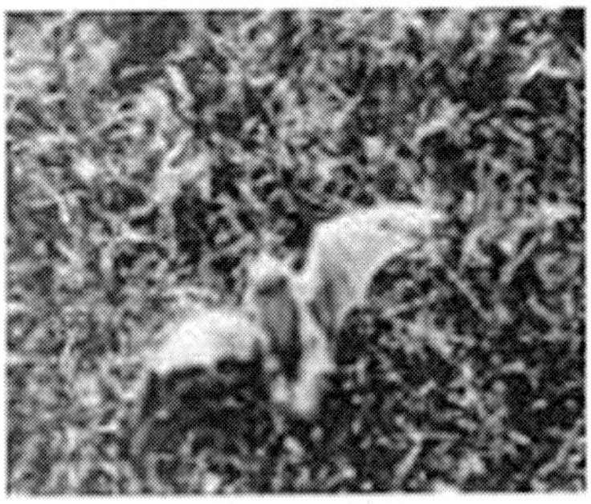

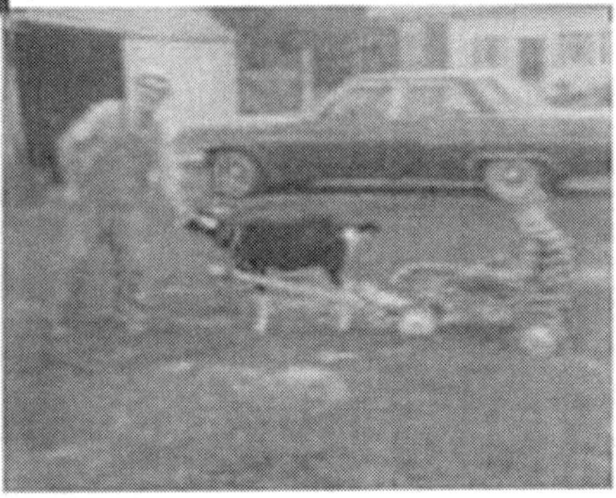

CHAPTER 7

Pets

Animals were a big part of my life while growing up on the farm. We always had cattle, hogs, sheep, and chickens. Mom took care of the chickens most of the time but I enjoyed gathering the eggs. It was also my duty to clean out the large chicken house about once a month, one of my least favorite jobs. Cattle were my favorite as they required less work. We also had two milk cows. It was always fun to be sitting on an old milking stool and squirt milk into the face of one of our cats sitting on the barn door ledge. Raising hogs in the era before confinement buildings was a daily challenge. You were constantly chasing hogs that had escaped from the pen, or fixing fence, or hauling water, or cleaning out sheds, or hauling manure, or filling feeders – you get the general idea. Work, work, work, mud, mud, mud.

I will never forget the day I foolishly attempted to walk across a very muddy hog lot carrying a 5-gallon bucket of corn in each hand through a herd of about 20 hungry sows. One of the very tame sows came from behind me running right between my legs. Buckets went flying and I rolled backwards landing face down in the mud and other stuff. You can understand why I don't have hogs today.

Pets played an important role, also. I had several, which included dogs, cats, rabbits, frogs, turtles, pigs, lambs, fish, an owl, a squirrel, two goats, two flying squirrels, two raccoons, and a snake. My adventure with the pet snake was a short-lived experience and due to my mom's influence, one that was never repeated. One summer my cousin Marsha, my sister, Karis, and I decided to walk down to the creek and swim in our favorite hole. We were all enjoying sitting in the cool water splashing each other when Marsha began screaming. She jumped up and started doing an unusual dance – like an Indian dance! My jaw dropped when she started grabbing at her stomach and began pulling down the strap on one side of her swimsuit. Marsha reached inside her swimsuit and flung something through the air. A large crawdad landed next to Karis, who then joined in to create a screaming duet. I couldn't stop laughing but was able to grab my towel and run toward home before they could catch me. I couldn't wait to get home and share with Mom and Dad our latest adventure. As I walked through the pasture, a snake rapidly slithered across the cow path I was walking on. Wow! What a neat snake. I had to run to catch up to the blue racer. I had never been able to catch one before as they are very fast. Finally, I threw my towel over it and was able to keep it confined in the towel until I reached the house. Mom wasn't as excited about the snake as I thought she would be. She informed me I would have to build a cage for it if I wanted to keep it.

"No problem, Mom," I replied, "I'll start right away." I put the snake in a gallon jar in our mud-room porch. Common sense told me I had to put something over the jar that would keep the snake in but would also allow the snake to breath. Being ten years old and in a hurry, I didn't exercise much serious thought with the issue at hand. I grabbed the first thing I saw, an old plastic funnel, and placed it into the jar opening. There! The snake had plenty of air to breathe. I rushed out of the house and found some mesh wire and old boards and worked really hard to build a cage for my latest capture. I couldn't wait to try to train the blue racer to run laps around the track. With the new cage in hand, I ran back to the house only to find an empty jar with the plastic funnel still sitting in the top. Uh oh – now I was really in trouble! Mom and I searched the whole porch but we never found the snake. Two weeks later in my bedroom, I opened a drawer of my dresser and there was the blue racer curled up on top of a pair of jeans. I knew the risk was too great to share my find with Mom. Quietly I caught the snake and slipped outside, releasing it in the garden. Fortunately for the snake, he never reappeared while Mom worked in the garden. Mom had a wicked swing with the hoe.

Another unusual pet I had was a screech owl. When I was in 8th grade at Timewell Grade School, our class consisted of 6 boys and no girls. We were constantly looking for ways to distract each other in class, like throwing spit wads of paper at each other or shooting rubber bands at flies on the windows, without being seen by the teacher. One day while using the excuse to use the pencil sharpener which was on a window ledge (I was actually trying to retrieve some rubber bands) I noticed something unusual outside. There were some large maple trees in front of the school. In one of the trees, I could see a big bird sitting by a hole about six feet from the ground. After school was dismissed and with some assistance from one of my 8th grade buddies, we were able to climb the tree, reach in the hole, and pull out one of five half-grown screech owls. I gently placed the young owl in a traveling nest, my jacket, and sneaked him onto the school bus and went home with the owl. I kept the owl in a small chicken house and fed it raw meat for about a month and occasionally a mouse when I could catch one. A six-foot string attached to my wrist and his leg allowed him to fly a little and land on my arm. He never really tamed down much and seemed to like the flavor of my arm. I released him at the end of that first month but he stayed close to our house all summer.

That same spring I caught a bat and decided to take it to school and show everyone. If our bus got to school early enough, we could play in the gym a few minutes before classes started. When I got to the gym, of course, everyone wanted to see the bat, and of course, I was more than willing to show them. I opened the jar lid and out he flew. Needless to say, there were some screams, which scared the bat even more and increased the trouble I was in. All of my recesses that day were devoted to trying to catch the bat. He kept hanging on some curtains at the very peak of the gym ceiling. He finally flew out an open door after several of us threw rolled-up socks at him.

One spring day, I was in the hay loft throwing bales of hay down for the cows when I saw a large raccoon disappear into an opening between some bales of straw. I could faintly hear baby raccoons chattering under several layers of straw bales. Dad volunteered to help me catch one of the baby raccoons. We started moving bales of straw out of the way forming a square-shaped well, approximately 6 feet by 6 feet, around us as we went deeper and deeper toward the floor. There was only one layer of bales left and I knew the nest of coons had to be very close. Dad grabbed the strings of the last bale and lifted it gently. A very upset mother coon jumped out from under the bale and climbed Dad's leg, then went onto his back and finally jumped to safety above Dad's head. I don't remember what Dad said, but I will never forget the sight of him dancing around on loose bales of straw with a raccoon on his back! I adopted one of the baby coons as a pet and our whole family enjoyed Sally until the next fall. Sally wasn't content with her human family. When she got to be an adult, she chose to return to the wild to start her own family.

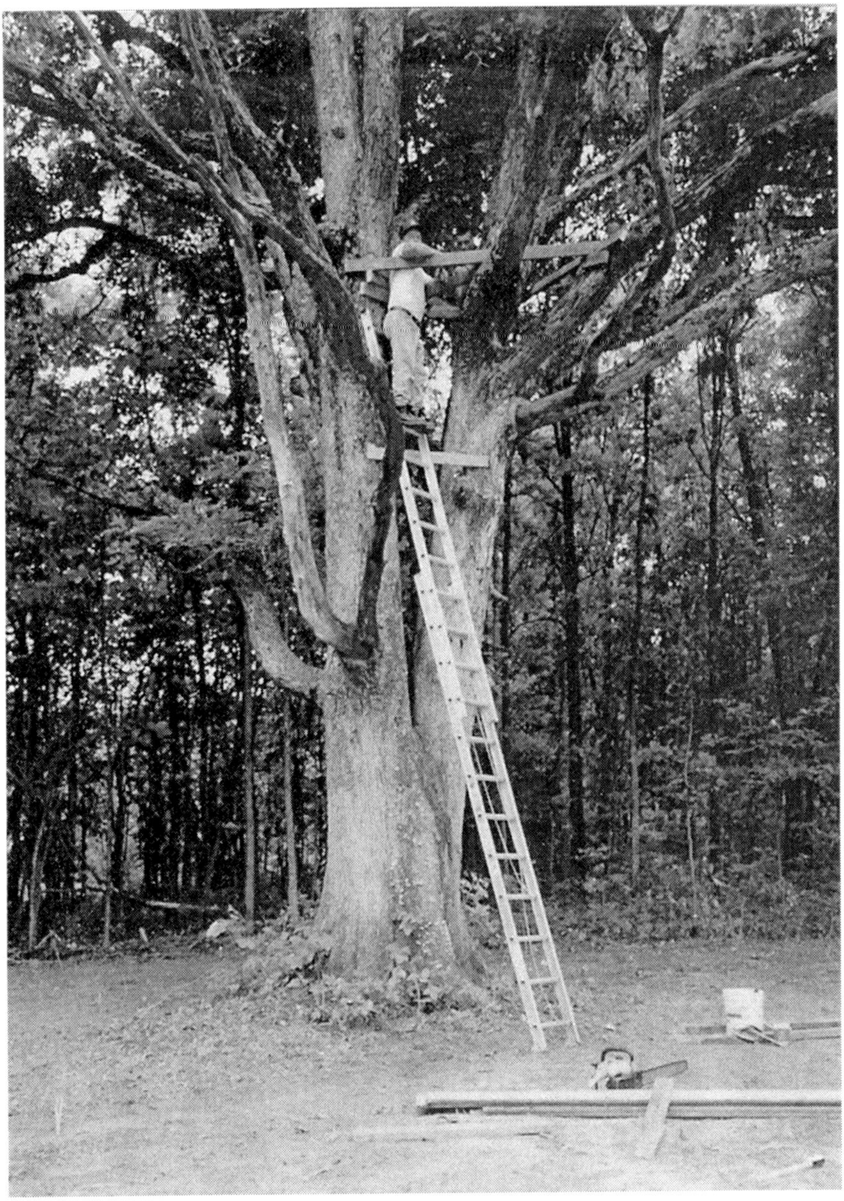

CHAPTER 8

Taj Mahal

Whew, I made it to the top without falling! The climb seems harder each time. Maybe my age is starting to catch up with me. Five years ago my wife and son helped me build my favorite tree stand. Our fellow hunters have referred to it as the Taj Majal. At the time, my wife thought I was absolutely nuts to build a platform in a tree over twenty-five feet above the ground. It was a difficult job, but my son, Andrew, and I enjoyed the challenge. The tree is a majestic white oak that is located in a narrow strip of alfalfa and orchard grass between a wheat field and thick timber.

It's quite a climb to the platform in the clouds. A combination of wooden steps, metal steps with tree limb steps in-between, but once you reach the top, you feel like you are on top of the world. The view is fantastic. This was so much better than the camouflaged pop-up blind I threw into the dumpster last week. I wouldn't have to worry about skunks up here.

The platform was apparently being used as a pit stop

by the local raccoon traffic. As I scraped numerous piles of droppings off the platform with my boot, my mind wandered back forty years in time to reminisce about my pet raccoon, Charlie. Our family lived in a very old farm house with a large basement where I kept Charlie at night. Dad used to get aggravated at me when, in the middle of the night, we could hear Charlie rolling an empty fruit jar across the concrete floor. I can still remember that sound echoing through the open registers.

That summer, Charlie and I were inseparable. He loved to ride with me when I drove Dad's pickup. Charlie would hide under the seat until I started the truck, then he would climb up the back of the seat and lay on my shoulders. He could feel the wind blowing through the open window and was able to look at the scenery as we drove down the road. Memories of Charlie will always be special to me, but Flash Jones probably still has flashbacks of Charlie.

Charlie was in his usual spot as I drove into town. Seeing all the other vehicles and people must have made him nervous. He climbed down under the seat. Dad had asked me to stop at the Dunbar Shell station and have Flash fix a front tire that had a slow leak. I won't reveal Flash's real name. The name Flash seems to hit the nail on the head because he was the fastest tire man around. I pulled into the driveway and shut the truck engine off, completely forgetting about Charlie.

Flash was sitting in an old metal chair by the pop machine when I walked into the station and told him about my tire problem. "Ain't no problem," he replied, "I can have that tire fixed before you can drink a soda."

Taj Mahal

Flash climbed into our truck to drive it into the open garage bay as I dug into my pocket for a dime. Flash didn't win that bet and I didn't get my soda either. I didn't know that Dad's pickup could burn rubber like that. I guess I should have told Flash about those worn brakes, too. Charlie didn't mean any harm. When the truck started, he just climbed back up to his favorite spot and onto an unsuspecting pair of shoulders.

I'm sure glad those two barrels of used oil and Flash's big Craftsman tool chest were parked between Dad's truck and the garage wall! They probably kept the building from collapsing. I don't know why Flash didn't have the bung holes on those barrels shut. It sure did make a mess when that oil shot all over the bay and Flash's Craftsman tools. Flash shot out of the truck like greased lightning and accelerated when he landed on the oil-covered floor. Remember those yellow metal racks that held every size of wiper blades from a VW Beetle to a Mac truck? Well, that's what saved Flash from the tire-changing machine. You just had to be there to understand how tense the atmosphere was. It didn't help any when a gas customer came in and saw Flash sitting in a pile of oil and wiper blades. The customer laughed so hard, he was on his knees with tears rolling down his cheeks.

Dad thought it was a good idea to leave Charlie home the next time I went to town. I never went to the Shell Station again, but I heard that customers had to drive their own vehicles into the shop from that day on. Those were the days!

Now back to my deer hunting. My platform was nestled between three huge limbs extending from the trunk of the tree. After years of hunting from this lofty height, I felt comfortable sitting there on an old kitchen chair. I didn't even bother to look into the large hole that was in the limb directly behind me. I had looked into it a couple of times in the past and had only found acorn shells and a corn cob.

I pulled all my gear up with a rope and settled in to wait for a big buck. That day was unusually warm and I noticed mosquitoes circling in for a free meal. Being well prepared, I dug into my backpack and found my camouflaged head net. Nothing would bother me now.

It wasn't long before several does and a spike buck appeared. I nocked an arrow and silently waited for the big one, not moving a muscle. Suddenly, some kind of tree monster with claws grabbed the back of my head. It's a good thing there was a big limb half-way down to the ground. I'm also sure there was a less painful way to land on a limb than one leg on each side.

Up to that point, I didn't know what kind of beast had attacked me, but when I hit that limb, a large ball of fur and my head net shot past me and hit the ground with a thud. I could see a tail with rings following that ball of fur as it ran across the wheat field. I could also see stars and red flashes of light and everything else associated with pain.

How could I get down without any more damage to my body and my pride? Five feet ahead of me smaller limbs branched out from the one I was embedded on. If I could scoot down to them and hold on, I could lower myself to the ground. I was just two feet from my goal when the limb I was on thought of a quicker way to assist me. CRACK!!

As I lay face-down on the ground, many thoughts went through my unstable mind. Most of them wouldn't be proper conversation. The ground almost felt good and I didn't want to move any of my aching muscles. That's when my cell phone started ringing. Usually I can't hear it in my coat pocket, so why could I hear it inside my backpack twenty-five feet up in a tree? There wasn't any way I could climb back up that tree to answer my phone and no one would have recognized my altered voice anyway.

The phone kept ringing and ringing. It suddenly dawned on me, the old saying that history tends to repeat itself. I'm now positive that if I had been able to climb back up the tree and answer the phone, I would have heard Flash's voice say, "We're even now, Old Buddy!"

CHAPTER 9

Buddies

It's time for a break. Just reminiscing about all the pulled muscles and bruises makes me sore. This would be a good time for some of my friends to step in and carry some of the load. One great example is John. His full name is John Wayne Henry. While in high school, I was a 130 pound pipsqueak. John was about twice my size so I called him "Big Bad John." Actually, John didn't have a mean bone in his body. As sophomores, John and I finally had a chance to go deer hunting together. We decided to wear brown coveralls with small orange hunting vests, hoping that we would blend in with the trees and become some-what camouflaged.

John is color blind so I guess I should not have been surprised when he showed up in coveralls that were bright red! With the orange vest and hat on, he resembled a giant clump of chili peppers walking around on the white snow. So much for being concealed!

John was very fortunate that day, though. He shot his very first deer but caught the worse case of buck fever I had ever witnessed! When I found John standing by his 8-point buck, John couldn't talk, let alone walk. That giant clump of peppers was shaking so bad his hat fell off.

The next fall, John and I had a chance to go deer hunting with some coyote-hunting buddies of mine from Timewell. Coyote hunting in our area was, and still is, very popular. Hound dogs are used to chase the varmints and then hunters in trucks equipped with CB radios attempt to keep up with the chase, hoping to eventually shoot the coyote. Everyone is given a CB name, not by their own choosing, but by the rest of the group. On that particular day, John and I were hunting with JW, Wiley, Black Beard, Sitting Bull, Little Richard, and Robin Hood. John and I were unanimously chosen to make a drive for the rest of the group. I think we young guys being chosen had something to do with John's red attire. John and I made a long drive through the timber and finally heard shooting ahead of us. When we finished the drive, we found JW field-dressing a deer with a brand new knife that he had made.

Have you ever noticed that it is usually the stronger people that have the weaker stomachs? John disappeared from the scene until the deer was dressed and loaded in the truck, out of John's sight. We all gave John a hard time about getting queasy, but John said he never actually got sick.

Before making another drive, we decided to eat lunch. Sitting Bull had brought a loaf of bread, a couple pounds of bologna, and a block of cheese. We were all hungry and enjoyed our simple fare. John was eating like a lumberjack. He was on his second sandwich and accepted another piece of cheese from JW when he realized that JW had sliced all the cheese with the same new knife that he had dressed the deer with! It's amazing how much faster ones lunch can come up than it went down.

Speaking of up and down reminds me of the time John took a good buddy carp gigging. In the early spring when the Illinois River was high, water would back up into fields and trap numerous fish in the low-lying areas of the river bottoms. The majority of these were carp, which are much easier to spot as they tend to break the surface of the water more often than other species. All of these fish in shallow water presented a good opportunity for archers and giggers to fill a bucket of good-eating fish.

John grew up next to the river bottom and had gone carp gigging numerous times. John's favorite weapon was a potato fork. The handle, similar to a spade handle, was easy to hold and due to its shortness, easier to aim toward a potential target. The flattened points seemed to hold the fish once it was speared, better than a pitchfork with round points.

John's friend, Clifford, had never been carp gigging and thought John was crazy to even suggest going. He said, "Why would someone walk out into knee-deep murky water, probably teaming with snakes, carrying nothing but a potato fork? Potato forks are for digging potatoes."

John pleaded his case and finally convinced Clifford to try it one time.

John and Clifford waded out into the muddy water

wearing shorts and old tennis shoes. Every weed Clifford's leg bumped into was a "snake." At one point, a small fish nibbled on Clifford's leg which resulted in Clifford trying his best to climb up on John's back.

Clifford finally settled down, and at John's suggestion, stood in one place for several minutes watching John. A large carp swam slowly by John's leg. With the potato fork poised like a spear, John was ready. With a quick lunge, he speared a three-pound carp, proudly showing Clifford his prize before putting the fish in a gunny sack. This successful action perked Clifford's interest.

"Ok, I'm ready to try it," Clifford said.

Several minutes went by before John spotted a large V appearing on the surface of the water. The V was pointed toward Clifford and was closing in fast.

"Get ready," John whispered, "It's going to go right by you."

Clifford raised his potato fork as John had done. The V instead of going past Clifford, went right between his legs. Clifford yelled and speared at the same time. Then he accelerated his yelling as he had speared his own foot. To Clifford's adamant objections, John's common sense told him they had to get that fork out of Clifford's foot before they could move. Grabbing the lower part of the potato fork with both hands, John jerked up at the same time Clifford leaned forward. The handle of the potato fork caught Clifford above the right eye. This move stopped Clifford's yelling and it also put them both in the water. Clifford was on his back with John on top. Clifford was sputtering muddy water and blood was running down his face as John helped him to his one healthy foot. They hobbled back to the truck like contestants in a 3-legged sack race.

That was the first and last time Clifford ever went carp gigging.

Did I mention Black Beard? Black Beard was more or less the leader of our rag-tag hunting group. There are two incidents that I recall that involved Black Beard.

I have enjoyed breaking in a new pick-up truck only twice in my life. In 1978, we were coyote hunting close to Siloam Springs State Park. Black Beard was walking down a snow-covered gravel road when I spotted him. I drove down the road in my new Ford pick-up and asked him if he wanted a ride. Black Beard had mud all over his boots, so he decided he would ride in the back of the truck. Black Beard stepped over the tailgate and took 2 steps forward. I happened to be watching in my rear-view mirror when Black Beard's muddy feet flew up off that ice-covered slick floor. Black Beard's body levitated in the air even with the top of my cab for about a half a second. Then it looked exactly like one of those pick-up commercials where they drop a ton of concrete blocks from the boom. The word "boom" isn't a very good description of Black Beard's landing. It was more like sawing a large oak tree down and hearing it land on a frozen lake. I jumped out expecting the worse. Before I could even ask if he was alright, Black Beard just told me firmly, "Just drive me to my truck." He was much safer in his prone position so he just remained there.

When I got close to his truck, I pulled off the road but didn't notice that my truck was parked up hill. I was sure glad some of the other guys had witnessed what had happened and were close by to see if we needed any help.

Robin Hood walked up to the back of the truck at the same time I got there. We both looked down at Black Beard's reddened face. Black Beard didn't seem to appreciate the humor of the situation and threatened to whip us both if we cracked a smile.

Robin Hood said, "You better not try to climb over that tailgate again," and with that said, he opened the tailgate. Black Beard slid out of that truck like Chevy Chase riding down the snow-covered mountain on his polished disk. There he was flat on his back a second time in two inches of snow in the middle of four other hunters and two hound dogs that liked to lick faces!

In the late 70's, snowmobiling tended to compete with coyote hunting. The winters then were more like the old-fashioned winters with lots of snow.

To protect our day-time coyote hunting, several of the same group along with wives and children would ride snowmobiles at night. Several of us had paths through our woods and pastures and would meet for a group trail-ride once a week. This particular week it was our turn to host the event, so my wife had hot chocolate and cookies prepared. I had built a large bonfire in the alfalfa field close to the house. There was six inches of snow on the ground and it was a perfect night for riding.

Black Beard always had the biggest gun, the fastest truck, and his snowmobile was no exception. It was impossible to keep up with him. He would get ahead of everyone and then wait on us, sometimes kidding us about dragging anchors or peddling our snowmobiles instead of having motors.

On the last stretch back to our alfalfa field, Black Beard took off again and got completely out of sight. Now was my chance! I stopped all the riders and shared my plan.

When we got back, Black Beard was sitting by the fire drinking a cup of hot chocolate with the usual, "where have you been" look on his face. I thanked everyone for coming and suggested we have a race to the other end of the field and the loser would play host next week. Everyone agreed, even Black Beard, because he knew he would win.

There were nine snowmobiles lined up at the starting line. My wife, who was standing by the fire, dropped her arm to start the race. Black Beard shot down the field like greased lightning. He was flying so fast I was afraid he wouldn't be able to stop at the fence. We were so far back, it was hard to tell how close he came. In fact, we were still sitting on our snowmobiles at the starting line – we had never left!

Thank goodness it was cold that night. It probably helped Black Beard get cooled off some before he got back to the fire. The only thing Black Beard said when he joined us was, "One of these days!!!"

Dynamite was another one in our hunting group. He didn't have the patience that one needs to hunt 8 hours a day, but when he did come along, he usually made it interesting.

Dynamite wasn't a nick-name he chose for himself. Game wardens tend to be a more curious about characters referred to by that name. Dynamite earned his notoriety quite innocently. When Dynamite was in high school, one day he was rummaging through an old shed and found a half-case of old dynamite. He noticed beads of sweat on the outside of the wooden case. Being the practical person he was, he thought it should be disposed of. His parents weren't home so he relied on his own common sense. "If I blow it up on the pond behind the house," he thought, "I shouldn't have to chop ice at the pond for awhile. The cows would be able to drink water all week."

As you all know, what might seem like common sense usually turns out to be telepathic waves from an alien source bent on Earth's destruction.

Very slowly and carefully, he carried – yep, he carried – the old box of dynamite over slick lots down to the ice-covered pond and set it right in the middle of the pond. "Dad will be proud of me," he thought, as he got his dad's high-powered rifle out. Lying down on the porch of his house, he centered in on the box and fired. Neighbors thought the Enola Gay had completed a 2nd mission! Chunks of ice and dead fish were everywhere. Something that looked like thin pieces of ice were laying all over him on the porch. When he was able to un-cross his eyes and wriggle his ears back to their normal location, he observed his handiwork. No more chopping ice this week. When he turned around to take the gun back, what he saw made him wish he had ice to chop. Eighteen windows were completely blown out of the house!

One day the Timewell Wolf Pack, as we called ourselves, was hunting in the vicinity of Dynamite's house. We had several dogs out, one of which was Red, a three-legged dog that could outrun most of the other dogs. Our Wolf Pack had been small in numbers that day, but when the dogs got a fresh jump and, "Coyote spotted," was yelled over the CB, other hunters showed up in short order. Dynamite was one of these hunters and positioned himself somewhere in his pasture.

Little Richard, who was walking with the dogs, yelled on his walkie-talkie, "The dogs are chasing a deer," and he needed someone to get ahead of the dogs and catch them. It was Dynamite that replied over the CB, "I see two dogs running toward my truck. I'll catch them."

Everyone stayed off the radio hoping Dynamite could catch both dogs. It was several minutes before we heard him gasping for breath as he whispered into the mike, "huh, huh, one dog got away but I caught that one-legged dog."

After that communication, Dynamite was fair game. It was LBJ who had the quickest wit and asked in reply, "Was that dog riding a pogo stick?"

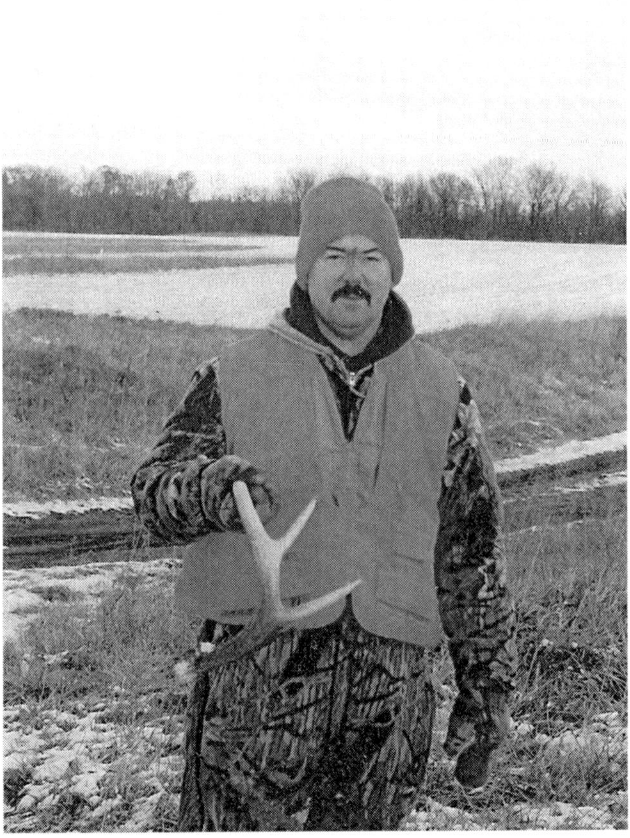

CHAPTER 10

Knothead

Otis is one of those unfortunate deer hunters that fate seems to frown on. You know the type: a huge buck is walking on a deer trail directly toward Otis who is hiding behind a tree 80 yards away. A squirrel up in a hedge tree chews through a hedge ball which drops directly onto the buck's back. The buck, sensing danger, disappears pronto! Otis is steaming mad, stomps up the trail muttering something about taking care of that blankety-blank squirrel. Otis, who is looking up for that pesky squirrel with his gun raised, steps on the hedge ball, loses his balance and falls flat on his back. As he stands up, he spooks another buck who was curious about the unusual pile of something lying on the trail. It didn't seem to matter what hunting tactics Otis tried or what products he used, big bucks were completely safe.

A few years ago, my wife and I invited the hapless Otis to hunt with us. We have an excellent hunting area and felt confident we could improve his success rate. Opening day, my wife had to work, leaving Otis, myself, and a nephew comprising our hunting group. It was very warm that day, so we decided to sit on stands. The deer weren't moving at all.

The next day was bound to be better. By noon on Saturday, though, none of the four of us had bagged a deer. Time to change tactics!

That afternoon, I placed my wife, Otis, and my nephew on excellent crossings. I would make drives toward the three hunters. Each of us had a cell phone to use only for important communication. At 3:30, I jumped several deer which ran directly toward the other hunters, raising my hopes. Patiently, I waited for 15 minutes, not hearing a single shot. Something should have happened by now. The deer should be in their laps! Fifteen minutes was as long as I could wait. I called my wife on the cell phone. When the phone rang the second time, Bam Bam Bam was heard in her direction. Instead of the usual greeting, "Hi," it was a garbled message of something like, "Thanks a lot! There__big buck__headed right___ me___the stupid___rang." Needless to say, I acted like I couldn't hear her and we didn't get any deer that day either.

The next deer season was in December. It was much colder with snow on the ground. The first day, my wife and my nephew were fortunate enough to fill their tags.

On Saturday, my wife agreed to walk with me. Maybe the two of us could drive some deer toward Otis who hadn't fired a shot yet.

We sent Otis to a strategic location and started our drive. Just ten minutes into the drive, I spotted a large buck sneaking through the trees in the opposite direction.

Apparently, Otis had jumped the buck while walking to his stand. The buck was limping badly so I decided to try a long shot. The buck dropped where he stood.

After tagging the buck, I dreaded the task of getting him out of the timber. The buck was on the side of a very steep hill in thick briars on the wrong side of a creek and a long, long way from our truck. My wife showed up and after high 5's, we decided to continue the drive toward Otis.

As you would expect, Otis saw absolutely nothing. When the three of us got back to the truck, another hunter stopped by to see if we had any luck. It was a big relief to us that he had a 4-wheeler in his truck and was willing to help retrieve the buck. The 4-wheeler was unloaded and the hunter drove it as far as the creek. The four of us crossed the creek and climbed the steep hillside to where the deer lay. After looking at our options, it was agreed the easiest route would be to drag the buck side-ways on the hill and through a woven-wire fence, then down the hill to the creek. Otis and I each grabbed an antler and dragged the buck to the fence. So far, so good. The helpful 4-wheeler owner stepped down on the woven-wire fence and lifted the barbed wire. Otis and I crawled through the opening. We then reached back through the opening, each grabbing an antler and attempted to pull the buck through the fence. Unknown to me, the buck's shoulder was hung-up on the fence, stopping our progress. I pulled with all my strength and suddenly found myself lying flat on my back holding an antler in my left hand, minus the deer.

"Are you alright?" asked my wife.

"I'm fine," I said, as I sat up.

Then we noticed Otis was lying face down in the snow not moving a muscle. We were terrified as we gently rolled over an unconscious Otis. There was a circular mark on Otis's forehead with blood running down from it over his nose. Being the helpful person that she is, my wife held a handful of snow against Otis's forehead to stop the bleeding, when he finally decided to drift back to the somewhat painful reality of the situation.

"Oh, oh, my aching head!" he muttered as he pushed a small pile of snow from his forehead. "What happened?"

Showing him the antler, I replied, "Apparently God was watching out for you, my friend! When that antler popped off the buck's head, it must have been traveling the speed of light when I fell backwards from pulling with all my strength. The round base of the antler must have hit you right between the eyes."

It was such an overwhelming relief that Otis was talking again. I shuddered to think what could have happened if the antler had struck him in one of his eyes. For some unexplainable reason, seeing Otis sitting there in the snow with blood trickling down from the round circle on his forehead, and holding a deer antler, seemed outrageously funny to the rest of us! Otis didn't share the humor but we laughed uncontrollably with tears running down our cheeks. During those few minutes, memories were frozen in time forever.

Eventually, the other hunter and I were able to get the 1-antlered buck back to the truck about the same time my wife and Otis arrived. I happened to have a camera in the truck and took a picture of Otis holding the antler that temporarily sent him to la-la land.

On the following Monday, it was back to work for Otis and I. We both worked at a correctional facility. After roll call was over, I showed the picture of Otis and the infamous antler to some of the other officers. A secretive plan was conceived by some of our fellow employees that had too much time on their hands.

The next morning in roll call, a memo was read by the shift captain stating that Officer Otis was receiving a special award. I noticed Otis stand up a little straighter, as he prepared to receive his award. Otis, who still had two Band-Aids across his forehead, was handed an important-looking manila envelope. His face turned red as he pulled out a wooden plaque that had a picture of him holding the antler. Beneath the picture were these words, "one deer permit $15.00, one box of slugs $2.00, being knocked out by a dead deer, Priceless!"

Fate did seem to ease up on Otis after that. The next year, I drove a nice buck toward Otis. He decided to pass up on the buck thinking it was too small. On second thought, he shot it at the last possible moment. It turned out to be a large, 8-point with a 24-inch spread.

With a reputation as well-known as the one Otis possesses, I think he should be unanimously accepted into the Timewell Wolf Pack with the name, "Knothead!"

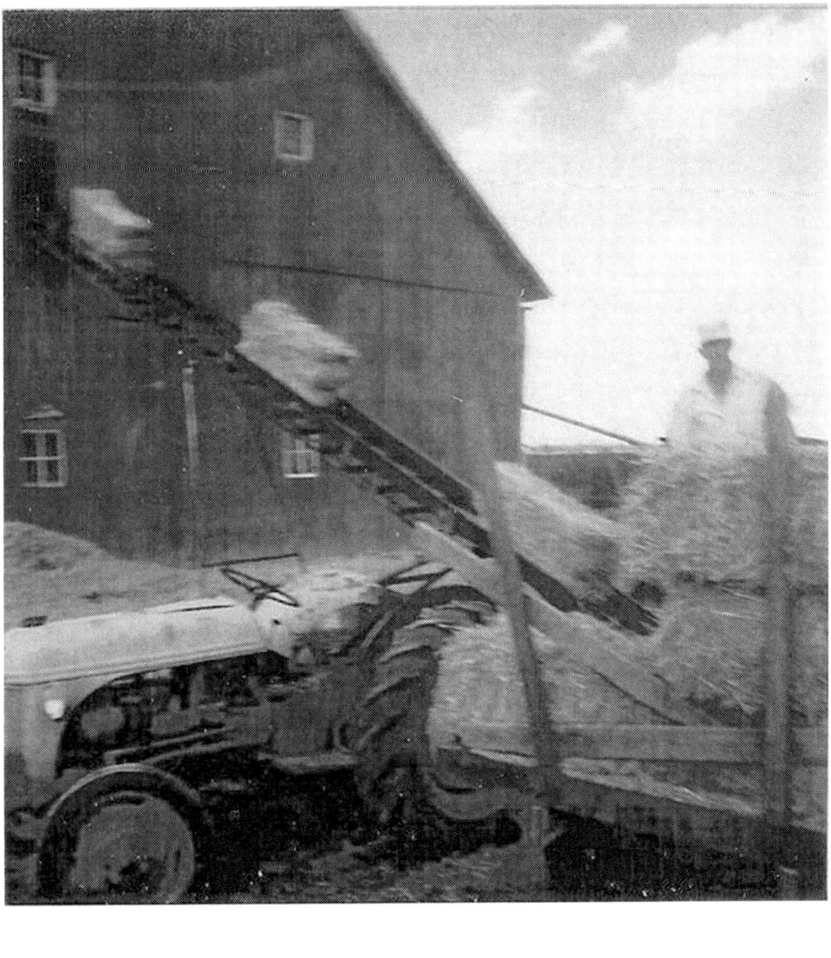

CHAPTER 11

Hay, Hay, Hay

In my younger days, baling hay was just as much a part of growing up as playing ball. Every farm boy around spent most of the summer months bucking bales. Even boys who lived in town worked right along with us earning a few extra dollars. Most of those dollars were spent in town on Saturday night or at the annual Brown County Fair.

There wasn't anything easy about baling hay. It always seemed like whoever you worked for chose the hottest day to bale. If you rode the wagon behind the baler, it didn't matter where you stood, the hay dust always blew into your face. After a full day of riding that wagon, you felt like you had eaten as much hay as a cow would all winter. The fields were usually so rough that you learned to bend your knees slightly to absorb the bouncing, like shock absorbers. Of course, when the field was extra rough, you were either carrying a bale from the baler or trying to keep the other bales from falling off the wagon. My uncle used to enjoy putting me to the test during conditions like this. He would stand up there on his Oliver tractor, smile at me, open the throttle a little more, and yell back, "We've got to get this field done before it rains." Of course, there was hardly a cloud visible anywhere. The bouncing wasn't as noticeable to him on the tractor. He would stand on his left foot with his right foot on the tractor seat and steer with one hand. This way, he could watch the baler easier and even glance at me once in awhile.

I used to envy him as I watched from the wagon between bounces. He was so relaxed, he could roll a cigarette with his free hand. Someday, I hoped to have my own tractor and baler, but I didn't have any inclination to smoke or chew tobacco like my uncle. Like most farm boys during that era, I sneaked out behind the barn once with a cigarette I had found. The timing must have been right. The only sensation I received from smoking that cigarette was turning green around the gills!

My reason for developing a negative attitude toward chewing tobacco was much more memorable. One day, my uncle took Dad and I with him in his car to a farm sale. I had the whole back seat to myself and decided to sit behind my uncle. He had his window open and when I opened mine, there was a cool breeze. My uncle chose that day to chew a wad of Bull Durham chewing tobacco instead of smoking. After awhile, he decided to relieve himself of a mouthful of spit and worn-out chewing tobacco, so out his window it went. It cleared the side of the car, caught a gust of wind, and landed right in my face. That was the first and last time I chewed!

I haven't forgotten about those guys up in the hayloft.

Hay, Hay, Hay

Their plight was even worse than working on the wagon. When the bales fell off the elevator and hit the floor, small dust clouds would erupt from the floor causing the air in the hayloft to be saturated with dust. In between loads of hay, everyone looked for a door or window in search of fresh air. Your visibility was affected by all the dust and you risked stepping in the wrong place and losing your balance.

One summer, Leroy and I were stacking hay in my dad's barn. Under the hayloft where we were, there were two old granaries. One was used to store sacks of feed and equipment. The other one was an old oats bin that hadn't been used for many years. It still had a small pile of ancient oats and the whole room was filled with spider webs and dust. Our cats wouldn't even go in there! The oats bin was filled by using an elevator through the hayloft window. There was a trap-door in the hayloft floor over the oats bin that I had forgotten about.

Leroy and I were working as hard as we could carrying bales of hay where they fell off the elevator to the middle of the hayloft. The dust was getting really thick. I stacked my bale and took a second to wipe the sweat from my eyes. When I turned around, I expected to see Leroy carrying his bale, but Leroy had vanished! There was a bale of hay laying on the floor and Leroy's ball cap right beside the bale.

This happened about two months after rumors of alien abductions occurred in the area. I got out of that hayloft as fast as I could. Dad was outside running the elevator and he knew something was wrong when he saw my white face. Dad shut the tractor down and asked me what was wrong.

"They got Leroy!" I yelled.

"What?" Dad asked.

"They got Leroy – his cap is still on the floor!"

It was then that we heard moaning from inside the barn. Leroy came staggering out of the oat bin door, cobwebs, dust and moldy oats stuck to his sweaty skin. Dad and I doubled over with laughter but at the time, Leroy didn't see the humor.

The most enjoyable part of baling hay at our farm was going down to the old pond after we were done to wash off all the dust and grime. The first time Leroy helped us, we decided to go swimming. As soon as the last wagon was unloaded, we headed for the pond. Leroy didn't know how to swim so he balked at jumping off the end of the dock. I jumped off the end of the dock and immediately started dog-paddling.

"Come on in, Leroy," I said. "It's not deep. I'm standing on the bottom."

Leroy jumped in right beside me and disappeared except for that same old ball cap floating on the dust-covered water. I had an inner tube waiting for him when he surfaced. It took quite awhile for Leroy to smooth his feathers down after that.

Leroy developed into one of the top hay hands around. Good help gradually got harder and harder to find. Dad tried several different boys my age or younger from town. Some were excellent workers, some were average, and some should have paid Dad instead of him paying them. I remember one in particular. By this time I had my own

Hay, Hay, Hay

tractor and worn-out baler. After almost daily repairs, I was beginning to learn that there was more to operating a baler than just standing on the tractor and rolling cigarettes. You were not only responsible for getting the hay baled but you were responsible for who was riding the wagon.

Albert's first assignment with our hay crew was to work in the hayloft. After taking twice the normal time to unload a wagon, it was discovered that the only thing Albert was doing in the hayloft was pushing the bales off the end of the elevator. The bales were going to fall off the elevator anyway, so Albert's next assignment was to ride behind me on the wagon. There is an art to stacking square bales on a moving wagon and Albert didn't have it. Several times I had to stop and reload bales that had fallen off. After showing him some tricks, though, Albert started doing better. By mid-afternoon, we were producing loads of hay that made it to the elevator without falling off the wagon.

We moved to another field where the first windrow of hay was on a steep side of a hill. At the steepest point, a piece of wood went into the baler, sheering a bolt. The flywheel, which consists of a 200-pound round steel wheel at the front of the baler slid off the shaft, fell to the ground, and started rolling downhill toward a deep ravine. Soaking wet, Albert wouldn't have weighed 130 pounds but what he lacked in knowledge and experience, he made up for in stupidity. Albert jumped off the wagon yelling, "I'll stop it!" He was oblivious to my yells of, "No – No!"

Albert got in front of that flywheel and latched onto it

like white on rice. After he made two complete rotations, I shut the tractor off and ran toward the ditch expecting the worse. Albert crawled out of the ditch covered with mud from an old hog wallow. He stunk terribly, but that snaggletooth grin was back in its usual place.

"Guess I won't try that again," he said.

Even though he would have flunked any kind of skill test involving work, Albert was well liked. And after the flywheel incident, he was considered somewhat of a hero around the hay crew circuit.

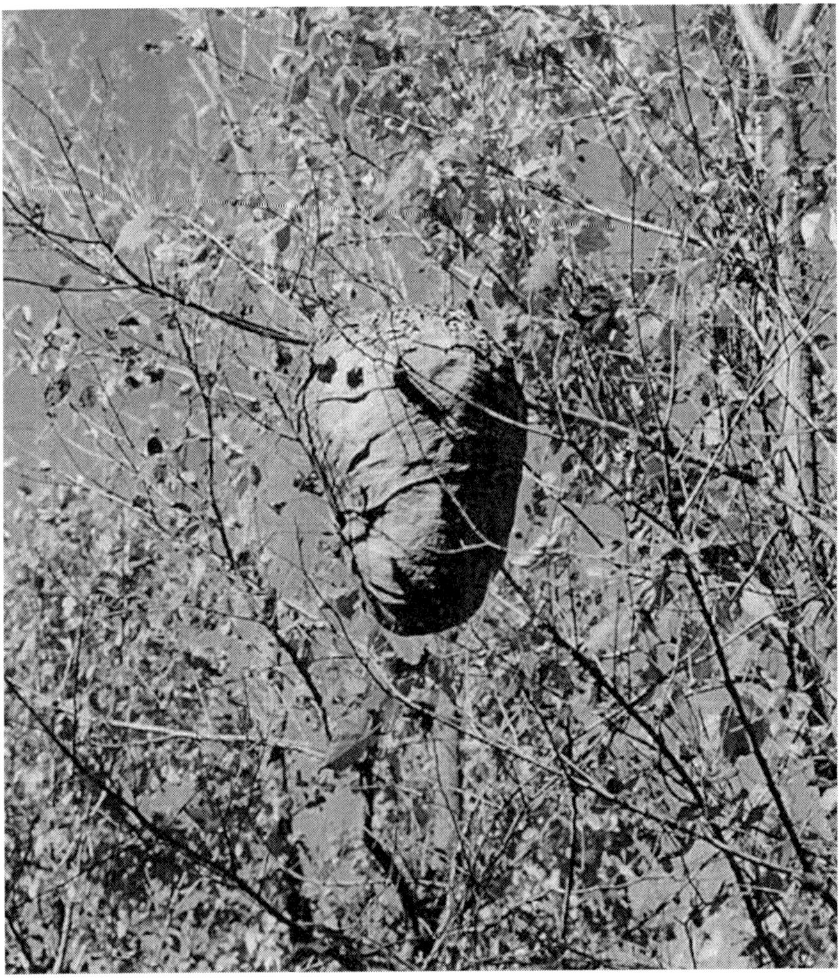

Chapter 12

The Hornet Nest

The hornet nest was enormous. Our neighbor, Pete, had found it while cutting firewood in our timber. My wife and I had walked into the woods to look at it and stood there in awe. Hornets were flying in and out of a hole the size of a man's fist. The lower lip of the hole was flattened somewhat resembling a miniature air strip.

"That's as big as the one that hung on your folks' porch," my wife stated. When she said that, a whole flood of memories washed over my mind.

In my youth, I spent most of my free time in the woods following my ambition of being a frontiersman. I would fish, hunt squirrels, rabbits, and mushrooms, anything I could think of for an excuse to be there.

One late afternoon as I was headed back to our house carrying two squirrels, I spotted a huge hornet nest high up in a tree. It was attached to a small limb which hung out over the pond. I guess this tribe of hornets wanted an ocean view from their condominium. Wouldn't Dad and Mom be surprised if I could get it down! It would look great hanging in our big house. I decided to come back the next day with the appropriate gear that I would need, although I didn't have a clue what one would need to harvest a hornet nest!

The next afternoon, I returned to the tree with a gunny sack, rope, and a hand saw. I sat down on a log and tried to come up with a brilliant plan while watching dozens of hornets flying to and from the nest. I sure wish Leroy could have helped. He had to go to the dentist and was going to miss all the fun.

I decided to tie the saw and gunny sack to one end of the rope and the other end around my waist. Leaving the saw and sack on the ground, I climbed up the tree until I was even with the nest. The climb wasn't hard, but I sure was getting nervous. The small limb that the nest was attached to branched off from a larger limb. The nest was about 8 feet out from the trunk. My plan was to work my way out on the limb, pull up the rope, carefully slip the gunny sack over the nest, and then saw the small limb that was holding the nest.

I made it about halfway out on the limb when a small problem developed. I tried to pull my rope up but could only pull it upward a couple of feet. Looking down, I could see what the problem was. The handle of the saw was caught on a small dead branch sticking out from one of the lower limbs. Good old common sense assured me that if I jerked the rope hard it would come loose. Common sense was right! When I jerked hard with both hands, that saw broke loose, shot up through the branches and the handle end hit the hornet nest dead center. Within milliseconds, I turned into a living dartboard

The Hornet Nest

with hornets all over me. I was instantly motivated into jumping out of the tree, landing in about 4 inches of water and a foot of mud. That's the first time in my life that I did a high dive.

Dad's best saw and the gunny sack were still dangling from the rope that broke when I ejected. Hornets were crawling all over the saw and sack venting their anger and sharpening their stingers for my next attack. "I gotta get Leroy to help me next time," I thought.

It was ironic that the next afternoon Leroy rode his bike up to our house. Usually I rode to his house as he had two younger sisters. The four of us, and sometimes other kids, would play softball in the sheep lot, the only space big enough to play. Sometimes you would have to remove black jelly beans that would stick to the ball when it hit the ground. Sliding into base was only attempted in important games where several kids were playing and the game was on the line. The bases were feed pans turned up-side down, so we always had to stop our game when Leroy's dad yelled, "Chore time!"

I knew Leroy wouldn't be eager to join me in my plan so I had to form another plan to be able to complete my first plan.

"Hey, Leroy, when was the last time you had some good honey?" I asked.

"Not for a long time, my folks can't afford to buy it," Leroy replied.

It took my best sales pitch to convince Leroy about all that delicious honey that might be in the hornet nest. I didn't know much more about hornet nests than Leroy did, but I had never heard of getting honey from one.

When we walked around the machine shed to pick up the gear I had stashed, Leroy pulled something out of his jeans pocket. "Look what I've got," he said, holding a half plug of Bull Durham chewing tobacco.

"Where did you get that?" I asked.

"Dad lost it this morning chasing our billy goat. He doesn't know I found it. Do you want a chew?"

"Na," I said. "I don't chew that stuff anymore. " I sure didn't want Leroy to know about my only experience with Bull Durham. As Leroy puffed out his chest and bit off half of what he was holding, I wondered if that was his first chew.

I picked up my bag of gear and we headed through the pasture toward the pond. I kept noticing the extra big lump in Leroy's cheek and wondered if he was ever going to spit. I was anxious to see if he had the same natural ability of his dad. Leroy's dad could nail a tumble bug on a cow pile ten feet away.

Right before we got to the pond, we had to climb the pasture fence. Leroy hooked one pant leg on the top barb and made a three point landing on the other side. I unhooked his leg, the fourth point, and he stood up minus the lump in his cheek.

"I swallowed it!" he blurted.

At that moment I felt closer to Leroy than ever before, bound together by an invisible bond that he knew nothing about.

When we got to the pond, I pulled an old inner tube out of the bag and also a two foot square piece of plywood. There was also a small bottle of gas and some matches.

"Ok, Leroy, I'm gonna put this inner tube on the

plywood, float it on the water and set it on fire. You use that long branch to push the plywood out directly under the hornet nest. The smoke will confuse the hornets. I will climb up and partially saw the limb. When the nest starts to swing down with the limb, you gotta keep the fire right under the nest. When the nest gets close to the ground, slip the bag up around the nest and hold the bag shut until I get back down. You got all that, Leroy?"

Leroy looked like he was in a trance but said, "Ok, I got it."

I started a fire on the tube and Leroy pushed it toward the right spot with the stick. The smoke billowed up toward the nest and there weren't any hornets visible. As I climbed the tree, I knew our chance of success depended on Leroy keeping the smoke under that nest. I also realized it had only been a week since I had tricked Leroy into an unexpected baptism.

Only one hornet stung me as I climbed up to the limb. Dad's saw was still hanging between me and the nest but I was able to retrieve it. I started sawing the limb where it joined the trunk of the tree. The limb started to give way.

"Ok, Leroy, it's starting to come down. Move the fire." The hornet nest was angling down toward the trunk of the tree and had cleared the smoke.

"Leroy! Leroy!" I looked down figuring that Leroy had left me to fend for myself, but there was Leroy on his hands and knees upchucking like there was no tomorrow.

Hornets were now storming out of the nest and getting even with me. For the second time in two days, I had to jump into the pond. This time, though, I made it into deep water but landed right on the burning inner tube. For a selfish moment, I forgot about Leroy until the steam and smoke cleared. Then I could see a swarm of hornets headed straight toward him.

"Run, Leroy, run!" I yelled.

I had never seen how fast Leroy could move. He looked like one of those exotic cranes that seem to walk on water. He even submerged completely under the surface for what I thought was a record time. When he finally broke the surface, he was smiling. "I can swim! I can swim!"

We sure had some explaining to do when we got home. Both of us were soaking wet and I had black rubber permanently sealed to the seat of my jeans. Mom and Dad were pretty understanding but I had to do extra chores for a long time. Leroy never chewed after that. Dad suggested that I wait until it got cold to get the hornet nest. It was as easy as picking an apple. That hornet nest hung in my folks' mudroom porch for 20 years.

"Are you going to try to get it?" asked my wife, bringing me back to reality.

"Are you going to help me?" I asked in reply. "Leroy isn't available and I need someone to hold the ladder steady."

"What does it pay?" she asked.

"All the hornet honey you could want," I replied.

As we walked back to the truck, I confessed to my wife about the honey, or lack of honey. She asked if I would wait until it got cold to get the nest.

"No, it would deteriorate if I did. How does tonight sound?" I asked. Although not positive, I didn't think the hornets would be a problem after dark. If we reduced the number of variables, the operation should be simple and safe. We would just use a step ladder, a large garbage bag, a small pruning saw, and a spotlight. One variable on which we refused to compromise was what we would wear. When I was a kid, I didn't have Carhartt coveralls or any kind of head nets. Being stung by hornets isn't my favorite past-time and I couldn't take any risks with my wife.

After supper, we dug out all of our cold weather gear and drove over to our timber. We put coveralls on over our boots and then tied binder twine around our legs. After putting heavy hooded coats on, we donned head nets and put on leather gloves. We looked like a couple of hillbilly astronauts on a moon walk! I picked up the old wooden step ladder and saw. My wife grabbed the spot light and bag and we headed out. We hadn't taken 20 steps before I was sweating. It was 60 degrees that night and 100 degrees in all of those heavy clothes.

The ground underneath the hornet nest was fairly steep so my wife would have to hold the ladder for me and also hold the light. As I climbed the step ladder it was becoming apparent to me that my wife was beginning to share the lunacy which placed me in situations like this. For her to even be here was a display of instability.

The eight foot ladder was rickety to begin with but my shaking knees made it worse. That's two variables we didn't plan on. Another one was our glasses fogging over from body heat. I could see almost nothing. And then there were the moths. They started flying toward the spotlight. My wife was having trouble with foggy glasses, also, and she thought the moths were hornets.

She started talking to herself, "Aahhhh, aaaahhh, aaaaahhh," and was waving the spotlight around like a flyswatter.

I finally felt the nest and was able to slip the large bag up over it. I took another step higher and started sawing the limb above the nest. My wife screamed and let go of the ladder. A large moth had somehow gotten inside her head net and was flapping against her face. You have to know my wife's fear of bugs to realize the gravity of the situation. I couldn't look down and couldn't have seen anything anyway in the dark. But I could hear her screams as she was trying to tear her coat and head net off.

I was still standing on step number seven of an eight-step ladder with a hornet nest in my hands. The ladder was shaking badly, probably from the influence of my vibrating knees. It would just be a matter of time before that ladder would give 'way leaving me hanging on a limb with the nest.

I was proud of my wife that night. She had more grit than Leroy. She finally shucked enough clothes off to get rid of the moth and steadied the ladder. I was able to saw the limb through and hand her our prize, a complete hornet nest inside a garbage bag. Of course, when my wife accepted our prize, the ladder and I went flying. Thank goodness for all of those heavy clothes I was wearing.

My wife and I sat on the ground for several minutes to cool off and silently reflect on what we had just accomplished. My wife was still holding the garbage bag by the top and didn't notice a hornet that had found a way of escape and was sitting on her hair. It was poised as if ready to strike.

"Hold still, honey, there's a stick in your hair," I said. I reached over and grabbed the critter in my leather glove, not showing her what it was.

Once in a great while, wisdom doesn't elude me.

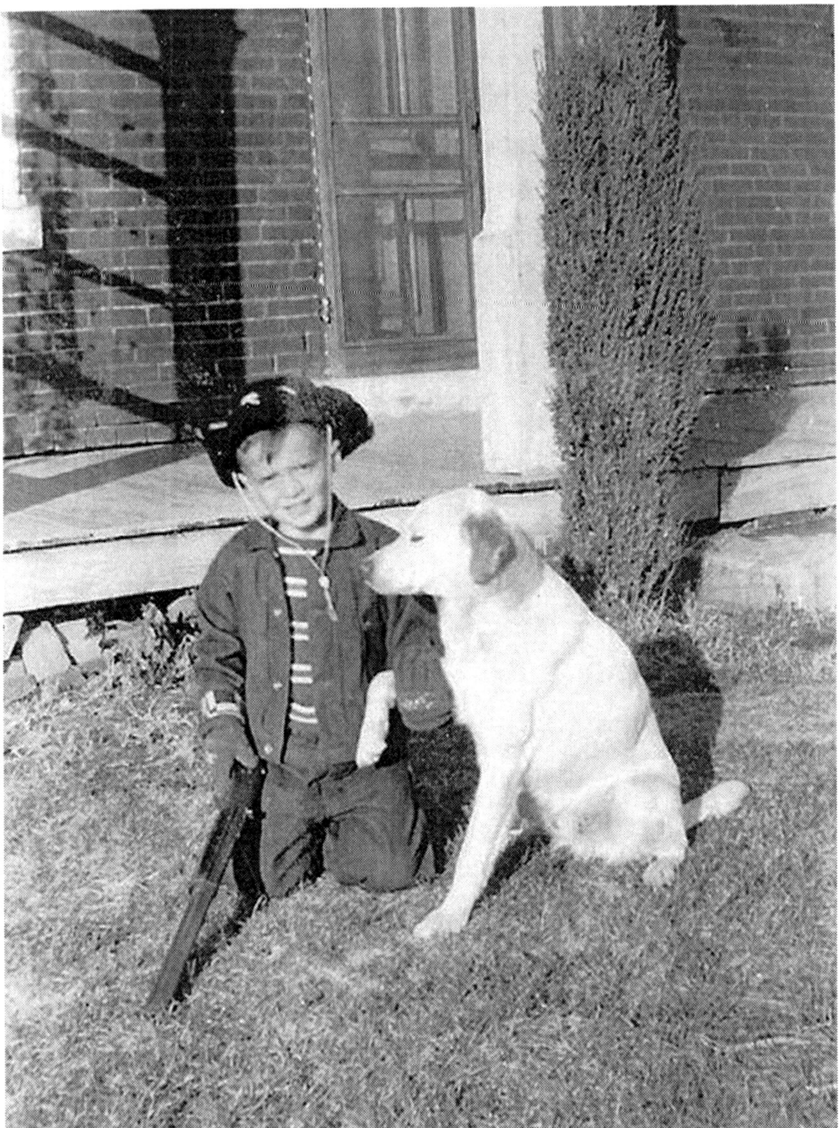

CHAPTER 13

A Promise Kept

Mom, Dad, and my two sisters have always claimed that I had a 1-track mind when I was growing up. At family reunions, they would always bring up evidence to prove their theory. We won't ask my wife and children if that is still true today.

For my Christmas present when I was seven years old, I was given what most boys at that time dreamed about, a Daisy BB Gun! Looking back, I realize now how huge a gift that was. Mom and Dad made sure we always had plenty to eat and warm clothes, but it was unusual for them to have extra money for new gifts.

At the time, I had measles and Mom wouldn't let me go outside to shoot my new gun. I was like a man in prison. I wanted to get outside so bad, I was driving my parents and sister crazy. I even told Dad that if I could go outside with my gun, I could provide fresh meat for the kitchen table.

Our house was ancient and had huge rooms. Mom finally allowed me to set a cardboard box in front of our living room door. Mom helped me draw a bulls eye on the front of the box and said I could shoot as long as I didn't miss the box. For two days I shot that box never missing. When I ran out of ammo, I would just pick BB's out of the front of the box and several would be lying inside. My sister, Karis, was even allowed to shoot a few times.

By the second afternoon, the front of the box had almost disappeared. I kept picking up little pieces of cardboard in the living room before Mom saw them. Sometimes when I shot, BB's would bounce back toward me. I finally asked Mom if I could replace the box. When we moved the shot-up box, we found that the wooden door looked like a flattened golf ball! Although the dents were concentrated in a 1-foot circle, there were dents on top of dents and a few BB's still stuck in the door. I knew Mom must have been really steamed at me but she never said a word. Needless-to-say, the indoor shooting gallery was closed forever.

Mom was very creative. We painted the door but before the paint dried, she held an empty tin can and pushed the bottom of the can against the door all over it. This created an unusual circle pattern. It didn't hide my art work completely but it seemed to diminish the bulls eye affect.

At the age of ten, all I could think about was becoming a famous frontiersman and trapper like one of my ancestors, Daniel Boone. Girls hadn't entered my future plans yet. You just couldn't go into the forest tracking a grizzly bear with a girl tagging along in a skirt and white bobby socks! I continually dreamed of living in the woods and living off the land. Uncle Harry would give me his copies of "Outdoor Life" and they were much more important to me than math and history books.

By the time I was eleven, it was apparent to Dad that I was a natural-born woodsman. One day we were building fence in our pasture next to the woods. Tippy, the best little hunting dog a kid could have, started barking down by the creek. I asked Dad if we could go check on Tippy because I knew he had some animal treed. When we got there, we found Tippy barking at a large groundhog about 8 feet up in a tree.

"Ok, Daniel Boone," Dad said. "Why don't you climb that tree and push him out?"

I couldn't back down from a challenge like that! If Daniel Boone could kill a bear when he was only three, surely at eleven I could climb a tree and show Punxatawnee Phil who was boss!

Up the tree I started, but when I got close to the varmit, he climbed higher. The higher I climbed, the higher Phil climbed and the more nervous I became. The tree seemed to shrink in size and the groundhog now looked more like a bear to me.

Finally, when the long-toothed monster realized he couldn't climb any higher, he changed tactics. Down the trunk he came right toward me! I shinnied down the trunk as fast as I could go, but Phil was twice as fast and mad. When he was within two feet of my head, I knew this was the end. I closed my eyes yelling as loud as I could, expecting those long teeth to sink into my nose. There were no teeth and when I opened my eyes, there was no Phil either! The groundhog had climbed down right over my arm and disappeared in a hole at the base of the tree. There were tears in my eyes when I reached the ground. Dad sure was worried about me, too, because there were tears on his cheeks when he stood up and regained his composure.

That winter I felt it was time to start trapping for my own fur. My first opportunity came when I noticed several coyote tracks in the snow coming and going through one of our pasture gates. I set two of Dad's metal traps in line with the tracks and covered them with loose snow and food scraps. I couldn't sleep very well that night because I was sure there would be a large coyote there in the morning.

Morning finally came and Tippy and I ran out to the pasture gate. When we got there, all we found were some black feathers scattered over the snow and a pair of crow's feet by one of the traps that had been sprung. Apparently, I had trapped a crow and Mr. Coyote had a supper of food scraps and crow.

Dad sensed my disappointment, so that night at supper, he promised he would skin the first furry animal I brought home. Dad would regret that little promise, but that promise made a large impact on my life. Sis was old enough to drive and on Sunday evening, she escorted me to Timewell to attend BYF (Baptist Youth Fellowship). After BYF was over, we headed home in our family's Rambler station wagon.

Three miles from our house, I spotted a large skunk ahead of us crossing the gravel road.

"Hit it, hit it," I yelled. All I could think about was that beautiful fur that would be worth a lot of money. That's my excuse, but to this day I still don't understand why my sister listened to me. She actually hit the skunk!

I was sure proud of her, being able to hit a moving target on a gravel road and not lose control of the car. Awesome!

"Stop the car," I yelled! Karis had to be in shock because she actually stopped the car.

I ran back and almost gagged when I picked up the limp skunk by the front foot and carried it back to the car and laid it on the back floor-board. As we drove home, all I could see was that beautiful fur on the wall. Actually, all that both of us could see were tears as we rode home with all of the windows open in 20 degree temperature! Dad would be so surprised! I couldn't wait to show him. Karis kept mumbling something to herself about Mom and Dad killing her!

She wouldn't talk to me even though I complimented her on her driving ability. As soon as we got home, Karis went running into the house and straight to her room. Dad wasn't nearly as happy as I thought he would be, especially after I told him how good Sis was at driving. I learned a lot about shampooing carpet, but we couldn't completely get rid of the odor. We finally put some kind of smell-good stuff on the floorboard and traded the car for another one.

What still impresses me today is that Dad kept his promise. He took care of that smelly skunk with no complaints. I now had my first fur and sold it for $0.50! That was the extent of my fur trapping career.

Sis learned that it wasn't always wise to listen to her younger brother, but we both cherish the memory of Dad keeping his promise.

CHAPTER 14

Stupid Is As Stupid Does

We have all made mistakes, right? Well, the one I'm about to share with you would get very high marks in the category of stupidity. I'm sure recalling this episode will cause personal problems for me and possibly great bodily harm. My wife has yet to get her revenge!

Shortly after Cindy and I were married, we moved to a small farm that we rented south of Timewell. We both had farm backgrounds, so we were excited to be out in the country. We weren't excited about the house. It was very old with no insulation. Each winter, I would literally wrap the entire house in plastic and put bales of straw around the foundation. This helped cut the wind speed down inside to allow the curtains to hang closer to the walls. One winter, we moved our couch and TV into the kitchen and just heated our bedroom, kitchen and bathroom. Being a very old house, it was also a refuge for critters. When we moved in, I had to spray the basement for fleas and even caught a couple of salamanders in the basement as well. I was smart enough not to show these

Stupid Is As Stupid Does

to Cindy. With all the adversities, we were still happy to be there.

One spring day, Cindy was washing clothes and I was building fence approximately ¼ mile away from the house. Suddenly, I could hear her screaming her lungs out. I had never heard her scream and it scared me to death! Dropping everything, I ran as fast as I could to the house, expecting to see her lying on the floor with a broken leg or an arm cut off. I ran into the kitchen completely out of breath to find Cindy standing in the corner still screaming. She was pointing her finger at a spider on the floor. I realized later I should have been more kind and sympathetic, but at the time both kindness and sympathy were not within my mental capabilities. Humor also failed to surface. After stepping on the spider and realizing Cindy wasn't hurt in any way, I quietly walked out of the house and back to my fencing job thinking, "Someday, someday..."

Four or five years later, our Timewell Lions Club decided to have a haunted house in Mt. Sterling for a fund raising project. We rented a vacant old 2-story house and completely changed the inside for a very spooky effect. In the room that I was assigned to, my friends and I hung up some scary looking rubber bats and some black rubber spiders about six inches in diameter. As I was holding one of the scary-looking spiders, something clicked in my mind, "someday, someday..." A brilliant plan began to grow in my not-so-brilliant mind. After we finished the room that evening, I put an extra spider in my coat pocket.

When I got home, it was almost bedtime, so I told

Cindy I was really tired and was headed for bed. While she was in the bathroom getting ready for bed, I put the rubber spider on her pillow and covered it with the sheet. Cindy always pulled her side of the sheet down before turning off the lamp. For some unknown reason on this night, she grabbed her corner of the sheet and jerked it down more rapidly than normal. This caused the huge spider to leap off of her pillow and into her face. I'm surprised our nearest neighbors who lived one mile away didn't hear her screams. Our dog outside in the doghouse started howling. Guess who else was in the doghouse? I consider myself fortunate that she <u>did</u> allow me to sleep on the couch. As I left the bedroom, I could hear her mumbling, "Someday, someday…"

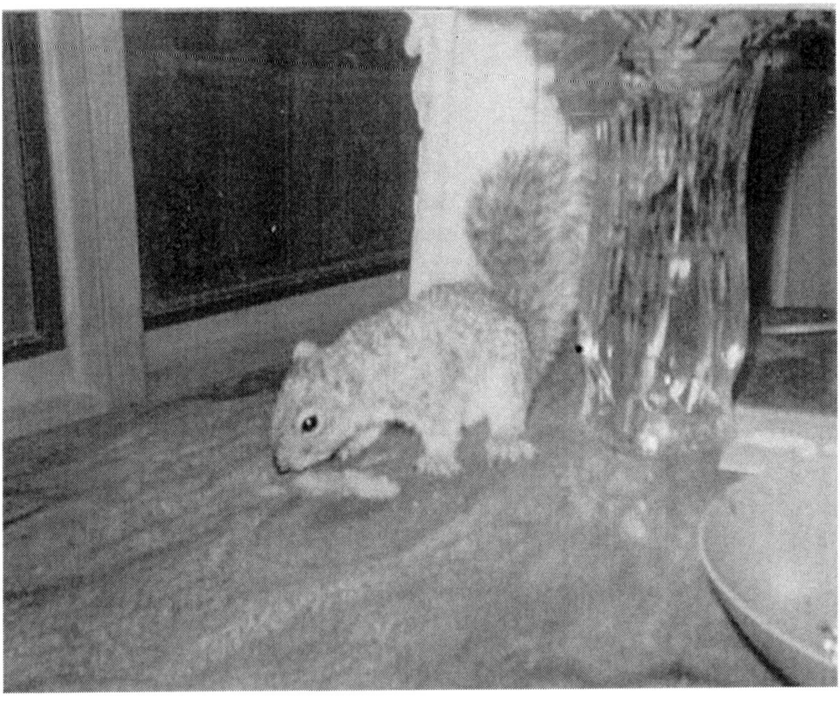

CHAPTER 15

Grunt

"I'll be glad when this is over," I thought, as Jim, the new insurance man entered our house.

I shouldn't be so negative. Insurance men have to work with so many different types of people and situations. I'm sure it is a hard and sometimes frustrating job.

As I followed Jim into our dining room, I couldn't help but notice his lack of hair, which reminded me of Grunt.

You might think that Grunt would be an unusual name for a pet, especially a squirrel. If you had been fortunate, or unfortunate enough, to have met Grunt, though, you would have agreed that our children named him well. Whenever Grunt got excited, he made a grunting sound like a small pig.

Grunt was introduced to our family when I pulled a muddy wet ball of fur from my coat pocket. I had found Grunt earlier that morning while feeding the hogs. He was lying in the mud and at first appeared to be dead. When I touched him, he moved a little so I gently put him in my pocket. I assumed he had been looking for something to eat and had possibly been stepped on by one of our hogs.

Grunt was in pretty bad shape but my wife and kids worked wonders with him. By the end of the week, he had revived and was a welcome little addition to our family. One of his favorite pastimes was to lie on the back of our couch and watch TV. There were a few times when my sanity was questioned about allowing a squirrel in our house. Like the time he made a perfect tunnel through the side and out the top of our son's 8th grade graduation cake! It's amazing what a little icing and a spatula can do. None of our guests that night noticed anything wrong.

Another time, he apparently had an enormous appetite for calcium as he chewed the longest point off the antlers of my former 10-point buck that was hanging on our living room wall.

My wife will never forget the night our 10-year old daughter, Rachel, had a slumber party with several girls. Grunt kept getting into their snacks so she thought she would catch Grunt and put him in a large bird cage that we used for situations like this. Grunt was in a playful mood and didn't want to be caught. My wife made a lunge for his tail as he climbed up the curtains in the living room. To the horror of six girls, two inches of Grunt's tail broke off in my wife's hand!

You're probably wondering why a bald-headed insurance salesman would remind me of an innocent little squirrel. I still chuckle as I reflect on what happened several years ago in our dining room.

After trying several locations, Grunt chose the curtain rod over the window in the dining room as his favorite place to dream about whatever squirrels dream about. Sometimes during his times of rest he would get hungry and run around the house until someone fed him a bedtime snack.

This particular night, a certain insurance salesman was making his second attempt to sell us accident insurance. His real name will be withheld to protect his honor and us from a lawsuit. For clarity, let's just call him Ralph.

Ralph sat down at the dining room table where there was enough room to spread all of his important-looking papers. Insurance has always been a foreign language to my wife and me; however, we did our best to act interested. Ralph didn't know that we had already decided not to change our coverage. Ralph wasn't the only one in the dark. None of us knew what was about to happen. We had not introduced Ralph to Grunt as Grunt had been asleep.

My wife excused herself for a few minutes and returned with iced tea for each of us and a small plate of cookies that she sat in the middle of the table. We will never know why - maybe Grunt was dreaming about his flying cousin, Rocky, or maybe he saw the cookies and thought Ralph's bald head was a large rock to land on. For whatever reason, Grunt jumped from his high perch and landed on top of Ralph's shining dome. Ralph had just put his glass of tea to his lips. Most of the glass of tea splashed into my wife's face and new hair-do. It was a full minute before Ralph outlasted my wife in a screaming competition. It was five minutes before I could pull myself off the floor and stop laughing. By that time, Grunt was nowhere to be seen, neither was my wife, and neither was Ralph. He didn't even bother to take his important-looking papers.

Today, as Jim and I sat down at the table with my wife, he asked the strangest question. "Do you have a pet squirrel in the house?" he asked.

"No," I answered. "Why would you ask that?"

"My dad retired from insurance last year," Jim said. "Mom and I have heard about him being attacked by a squirrel at your house probably 50 times in the last 10 years! When I became a salesman, Dad warned me to be careful at your house."

We didn't buy any insurance from Jim that night, but he seemed to appreciate that I referred him to our daughter and her husband who live close-by. As he drove away headed to their house, my wife asked, "Should we have mentioned our grand-daughter's pet squirrel?"

"Surely history wouldn't repeat itself," I said as I took the phone off the hook.

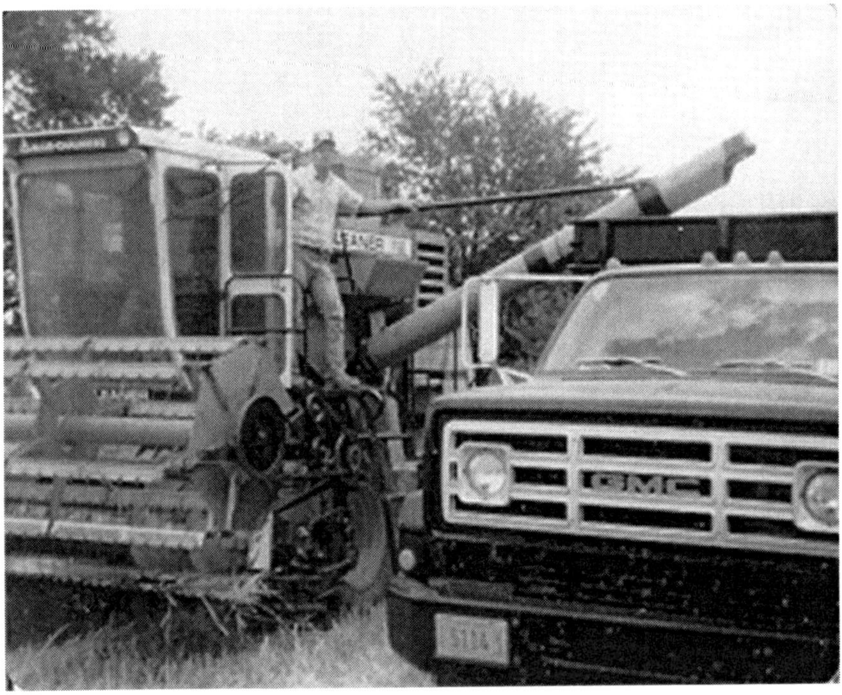
GMC

CHAPTER 16

Dreams or Nightmares?

Dreams are very intriguing to me. Why are we able to remember some of them and not others? It seems the older I become the more I dream about my parents and about my childhood. There are good dreams and there are bad ones, also. Occasionally, I have dreams from working at the prison. A few of those are nightmares. Our son, after returning from the war in Iraq, would literally jump up in his sleep and dive for cover. That's very understandable. Thank goodness his nightmares have faded away. Once in awhile I will dream of something to write about or something to build. It would be great to have those dreams more often.

Last week, I had what is for me, an almost normal dream. I was up in our old hayloft getting a bale of straw down for Mom's chicken house. When I climbed down the ladder and walked toward the outer door, a black panther lunged at me from the box stall where we milked the cows. I grabbed a pitchfork and hit him in the face. He fell back into the box stall, so I ran out the door. Mom was in the garden close to the barn, so I yelled for her to meet me at the garden gate. Close to the garden gate, I noticed a round metal hog feeder lying on its side. I opened the lid and pushed Mom in the feeder and then climbed in myself. We were able to rock the feeder until it sat upright and pulled the lid shut. There we sat. We couldn't see out and had no idea where the panther was. Then I woke up. How's that for strange?

I'm sure that stress and fatigue are major contributors to dreams or nightmares. Just recently, I dreamed that I was awake but couldn't move my body or talk! I finally woke up sweating and thought, "Wow, that was really strange!" My son and his wife described having similar dreams, so maybe I'm not so abnormal.

One dream I had, though, puts me well below average on a scale of normality. This is a true story and my description of it may offend some readers, but I refuse to apologize. Just keep in mind that life happens.

Did you know that one of the requirements to becoming a baseball player or farmer is having the ability to spit? Baseball players spit because they are bored to death. How many times have you seen a shortstop at a little league game or a first baseman in the major leagues adjust their cap, kick the dirt where they are standing, and spit into their ballglove. They then try to wipe the spit away with their other hand. Well, duh, if they spit somewhere else, their glove wouldn't get wet in the first place.

Farmers are more advanced in the art of spitting. Some farmers can hit a fly that is sitting on top of their own work boot, or hit a mailbox while driving a tractor down a gravel road. Maybe in some areas of the country where farmers raise unusual crops like rutabaga or cranberries, spitting isn't a common practice, but in Brown County, IL, spitting is as natural as a man cleaning the dirt out from under his fingernails with his pocket knife.

It always amuses me when at a large gathering like a farm sale, I notice young boys who act like they are professional spitters. ("I am a man now 'cause I can spit.") I think all farm boys go through that stage. Leroy and I used to have competitions in the sport of spitting. My mom was from Mississippi and some summers our family would drive to Taylorville, MS, for a family reunion. After a huge meal, one of the favorite past-times was having a serious competition of spitting watermelon seeds. We Yankees couldn't come close to the abilities of our Southern cousins.

There are very practical reasons for spitting. If you get something in your mouth that doesn't belong there, like a fly, or something that tastes terrible, you spit it out. Hopefully, not too many husbands have had to resort to this tactic when tasting their wife's cooking!

Other than chewing tobacco, the main reason farmers spit is because of all the dust they breathe. There was always dust in the air when raising livestock outside. Hog dust smelled different than cattle dust. Sheep dust was different, also, and I think chicken dust was the worst. Baling hay was one of the dustiest jobs on the farm, especially for those riding the wagon behind the baler. Every time the plunger would push hay into the baler, a cloud of dust would erupt. It didn't seem to matter which way the wind was blowing, invariably, the dust cloud headed directly toward the person on the wagon. You constantly had hay dust in your nose and mouth but you were usually so thirsty, you lacked the ammunition to spit.

As with livestock, each crop dust had a distinctive smell and flavor. Clover dust was very different from grass hay or alfalfa dust. Dust from harvesting corn seemed to irritate my eyes more than the others, but soybean dust was by far my least favorite. I wonder if soybeans and cockleburs are related? Those very fine particles of dust seemed to itch like miniature cockleburs. It would make your eyes water, your nose run like a leaky faucet and seemed to accumulate in your mouth like a snowdrift behind a picket fence. Just writing about my memories of dust makes me want to.....well, never mind.

I'm sure you're wondering where I'm headed with all my personal views of dust, spitting and dreams. Well, I guess I am trying to build a strategy of defense for my actions in the scenario I am about to share with you.

Back in the late 80's, we were having an exceptionally wet fall. Harvest was delayed by weeks. At the time, I was more actively involved in farming. With custom combining included, we had several hundred acres of crops to harvest. Finally, the rain stopped, the ground became solid, and harvest was in full swing. Being a late harvest, everyone involved in farming worked longer hours and pushed themselves to the limit. We were all concerned that the rains might start again.

Because of all the rain and the late harvest, the soybeans were twice as dusty as normal. Huge clouds of dust would hang around the combine as you drove

Dreams or Nightmares?

through the field. My old Gleaner had a cab, which helped a lot until the air conditioner quit working. After calling my local dealership, I was told it would be two or three days before they could repair it. We couldn't stop. I just added a lot more dust to my diet.

The next day was hot and dry, which allowed us to start combining much earlier than normal. The dust was much worse that day; it just seemed like a fog even inside the cab. I carried a short broom to sweep off the inside of the front window. It was hot in the cab so dust was sticking to my sweaty face. My nose ran, my eyes watered and spitting became an every-five-minute routine. Every few minutes, while driving with my right hand, I would open the cab door with my left hand and then hurl dust and saliva out the door. We harvested a lot of acres that day but by 9:00 P.M. I was drained. Bean dust itches so bad, it really makes you appreciate a nice long shower. But as all of you farmers know, it takes a long time to clear all the dust from your eyes, nose, and lungs. Maybe dust can be blamed for some of us being overweight today.

As soon as my head hit the pillow that night, I was gone into a quiet deep sleep until sometime in the middle of the night. Today, it is still as clear as if this happened yesterday. I remember starting my old Gleaner, lowering the bean head and heading down the rows of beans. At the five minute interval, I held the steering wheel with my right hand, opened the cab door with my left hand and hawked up the biggest wad of spit and dust I could muster and let it fly. That's when I woke up. I was sitting up, my right hand straight out in front of me holding an imaginary steering wheel. My left hand was holding the imaginary door handle and was also aimed toward my wife. Uh-oh! My final action suddenly dawned on me. I lay back down as quietly as I could hoping nothing else would transpire. WRONG! Cindy woke up saying, "Yuck, what's that on my neck?!!" I acted like I was sound asleep turning over on my right side. I could hear her grabbing Kleenex off the nightstand and then going into the bathroom to clean up. I expected a verbal attack when we woke up the next morning, but there was no mention of it. She apparently was too embarrassed to say anything. After all, she had eaten a lot of bean dust, also. Maybe she thought she was responsible for the glob on her neck!

It was months later and in a safe environment, actually at a family reunion, when I finally admitted that I was responsible for her wet, gooey nightmare.

Today, I farm much less than I used to and fortunately consume less dust. But when I see a farmer spit, it not only brings back memories, it also reminds me of one of the many adversities that farmers endure. I respect all farmers very much.

Sweet dreams, but always be careful where you spit!

CHAPTER 17

Sam

It was 9 A.M. and the chores were finally done. Now, to decide what to do: either cut a pick up load of hedge posts or load my 2-ton truck with square bales of hay. The next day, Thursday, would be sale day at the livestock auction at Hersman. The main function of the sale was to provide a market place for livestock and other farm-related items. It was also a social gathering place for anyone that wore bib-overalls or 5-buckle overshoes. Farmers from all over Brown County came to the sale on a weekly basis and always left with enough gossip to last until the next sale day. I really enjoyed going to the sale as it provided a way to earn some extra money.

The ground was muddy and I really didn't want to fight the mud in addition to the hedge thorns, so I opted to load by big truck with alfalfa hay. Although the ground was soft, I managed to back the truck up to the barn under the hayloft door. Hay prices were higher than normal, so I loaded extra bales. When I finished, there were over 100 bales on the truck with two layers of bales higher than the top of the cab. I tied the load down with ropes, and due to rain in the forecast, I parked the truck inside our machine shed. It was a good feeling to have the hay loaded. All I would need to do in the morning was jump in the truck and drive to the sale.

As I shut the shed doors, Sam, our family cat walked out of the shed. I grabbed Sam and scratched his ears and belly awhile before putting him down. Sam had been an important part of our family for over ten years and was still as playful as a kitten. Most animals have their own, individual personalities, and Sam was no exception. Sam's unusual habit was that he liked to climb up anything but was afraid to climb down. Several times Sam could be heard meowing loudly on the roof of our house. The extension ladder was carried back and forth from the garage so many times to rescue Sam, we finally left it leaning against our house. Twice, one of our boys had to climb the large maple tree in our front yard after Sam had won a climbing competition with the neighbor's Rottweiler. In cold weather, Sam liked to climb up under the hood of vehicles that had recently been driven. He would take a nap by the warm engine. As you can imagine, this often proved to be a harrowing experience, or should I say hairy experience. Actually, it was a hair-less experience as Sam lost the tip of his tail and half of his right ear when someone started their car before Sam was finished with his nap. After that, the neighbors probably wondered why we honked the horn before we started any vehicles.

The next morning after an early breakfast, I opened the machine shed doors and climbed into the cab of the

Sam

truck. I remembered to honk the horn before starting the engine. Everything was fine as I backed out of the shed and headed for Hersman. It was four miles from our farm to Route 24. Before pulling onto the busy highway, I stopped and tightened the ropes at the rear of the truck. I never drove my big truck over the speed limit so I was surprised when the first car I met flashed his headlights at me and waved both hands. The only thing I could think of was there must be an accident ahead. I slowed down to 50 MPH but started to get nervous when the next car also flashed their headlights. There must be a very bad wreck ahead or maybe the state police had set up scales. My load wasn't over the weight limit so I continued on. When the fourth vehicle I met at the edge of Mt. Sterling repeated the same routine, I thought that something must be wrong with my truck. The closest place to pull off the highway was at the Ready Mix concrete plant. I walked around the truck. The ropes were tight and the tires were fine. Although I had parked in a noisy place, I could tell the motor of the truck was running fine, also. Mt. Sterling was passed through with no further incident and it was just two more miles to Hersman. Maybe everything was all right after all.

Before reaching Hersman, another car and a pickup met me and both drivers were acting weird, waving and flashing their headlights. Had everyone gone completely nuts?!? Were they serving something at the auction besides the usual coffee and hot chocolate?

There were several farmers standing around visiting as I drove my truck into the area set aside for hay and straw. I noticed that two of them were pointing at my truck and laughing. Surely they weren't laughing at my load of hay. I always prided myself in the quality of the hay that I sold. Heck with them – I would unload my hay and leave.

After untying the ropes at the back of the truck, I carefully climbed up to the top of the load of hay. There, to my amazement was the reason for all the unusual attention. Sam was standing on the front bale of hay like a huge hood ornament. His front paws were wrapped around a string of binder twine. His hair looked like he had been cycled through a clothes dryer. There were two bugs stuck to his forehead. I reached down to pick up Sam and he was as stiff as a statue. I had to loosen his front paws from the binder twine. Even his meowing had diminished to a hoarse cat whisper. I carefully climbed down and set Sam on the seat of the truck. He didn't seem to appreciate the humor of the situation. After unloading the hay, I couldn't see Sam anywhere in the cab as he was hiding under the seat. I kept talking to Sam as I drove home. After parking the truck in the machine shed, I left the truck door open knowing Sam would want out when he was ready. The next day, I was in the machine shed and recovered the hay ropes from the empty bed of my truck. That's when I noticed a yellow streak fly out of the cab and tear out of the shed. Apparently, Sam thought I was getting ready to haul more hay!

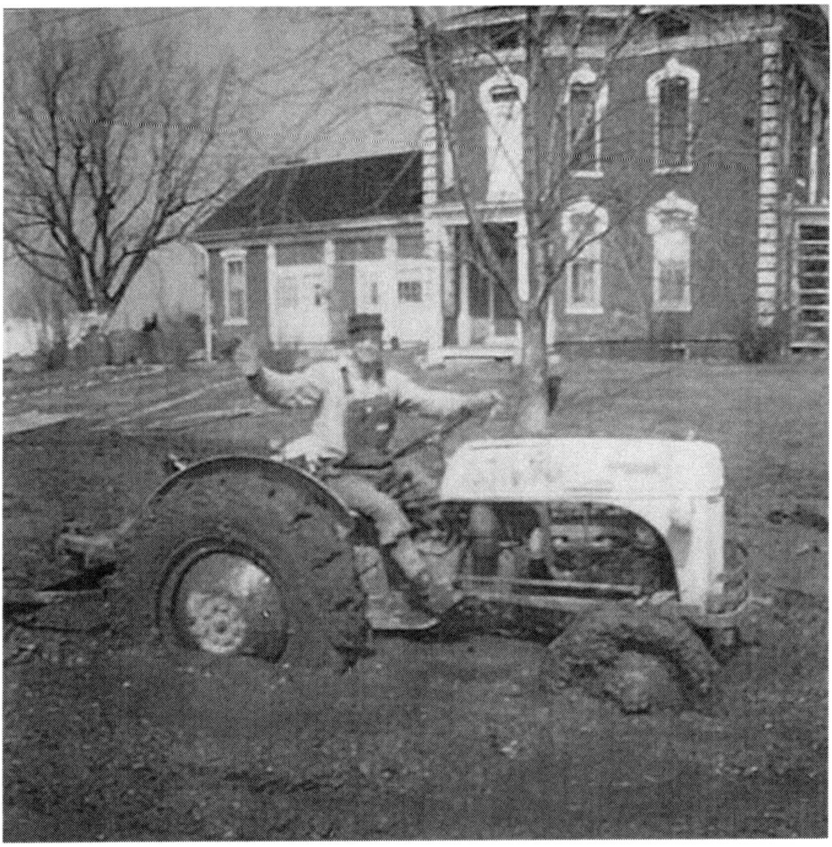

CHAPTER 18

Shoot Doggone

"Shoot, doggone," I said to myself as I put the truck in reverse and tried to get out of the ditch.

Most farmers have a favorite quote that distinguishes them from the farmer that lives down the road. For example, if you were at a large gathering and heard "dag nab it," you would know that my dad was nearby. Some of the quotes aren't printable and for the most part, don't make any sense. I don't remember very many that did make sense. If they meant something, you couldn't separate them from normal conversation. Take mine, for instance, "shoot doggone." What's that supposed to mean: shoot 'cause the dog is gone or shoot the dog 'til he's gone? I have no idea what it means but I started saying it at an early age and still occasionally say it if I miss a target or smash my finger. The most notable use of the phrase was unintentional at the time, but after the fact, seemed quite appropriate.

Several years ago, my young nephews Craig and Jeff were riding with me as I drove my pickup from one farm to another. Our neighbor's dog came out from nowhere and ran in front of my truck before I could stop. I felt terrible about hitting the dog but the neighbor saw it happen. He knew it was an unfortunate accident. Both boys were also upset at the time. Years later, Craig asked me if I remembered running over the dog and what I said. Memory is not one of my strong points. I had totally forgotten the incident. Craig said he would never forget when the dog disappeared down into the ditch and I said, "shoot, doggone!"

My friend, John's favorite saying was "good grief." I remember hearing it hundreds of times but never really paid any attention to it until now. John, I hate to be the one to burst your bubble, but "good grief" can only be a figment of your imagination. When you flip a coin, you're only going to get heads or tails, you can't have both. If that were to happen, we would still be waiting for the first Super Bowl to start. So John, why don't you just say "good." We've both had our share of grief.

Mom's identifier was "P'shaw." Who knows what it meant? I often wondered if it was something she wanted to grow in the garden.

Sitting Bull's was, "two in a hill."

"How're you doing today, Uncle Harry?"

"Two in a hill," he would answer.

That's the only one I could figure out. Old timers were doing a good job planting corn if they got two seeds in every hill.

So, I put the truck in low and tried to go forward one more time before giving up. No luck. I had done it again – I was firmly stuck approximately one and a half miles from our house. Two years ago, my wife had convinced me to purchase a cell phone for situations just like this. Of course, my cell phone was on the kitchen counter where I had left it. To me, having a cell phone is the same as taking the wonder drug Ginkgo Biloba to help your memory. I can't remember to take the pills. Is there another pill you can take to help you remember to take the first one? Anyway, now I had a long walk home to reflect on my driving ability.

As I walked past Pete's house on my way home, I started feeling better about my present situation, thinking back to when he got stuck 3 years ago.

On that particular day, I had just arrived home from work when Pete called and said, "I'm stuck. Can you pull me out with your tractor?"

I put on some warm clothes, hung a couple of log chains on the back of the tractor and took off. I stopped at Pete's house and he climbed on the tractor with me. "My pickup is about a mile back in the woods," Pete said. As we neared the area, we drove down a steep hill in the pasture. I turned the tractor around and backed toward the truck, trying to get as close as I could without getting stuck. It was early spring, and the ground was gradually thawing. Pete had driven his truck in with no problem early that morning while the ground was still frozen and loaded it with firewood. It had warmed up enough that when he tried to leave, the loaded pickup sank to the frame. Pete climbed down and waded to his truck reaching into one pants pocket and then all the others like he was searching for something. He turned around and walked back to my tractor. "My keys are back at the house." Knowing Pete the way I did, I didn't ask him why he would take the key out of a truck that was bogged down to the frame and then lock the doors. If anyone had found the truck they couldn't have taken it anyway!

After the scenic round trip to his house and back, we were finally ready to hook up the chains. Wrong, Pete pulled a small tow rope out and hooked one end on the front bumper of his pickup.

"Pete, we better use the log chains," I said.

"Nah, this rope is rated for 10,000 pounds. It's a dandy and will work fine."

Sometimes, the best way for Pete to try a different idea than his own is to try his idea first. In fact, it's the only way.

He hooked the other end of the tow rope to a clevis on my tractor. "Ok, Pete," I said, "We'll try it but I'm going to go real slow."

I drove forward to tighten the rope slightly and waited until Pete got into the truck. He started the motor to try to drive forward. I slowly moved forward, farther and farther away from his truck. The tow rope kept shrinking in diameter to the thickness of a carrot. I stopped the tractor but Pete motioned for me to keep going. I started moving forward again. The truck wasn't budging and now the rope was as small as your little finger. Something had to give – and it did. The metal hook on my end of the rope snapped. The rest of the hook attached to the rope shot like a rocket crashing through a headlight on Pete's truck.

"Shoot, doggone," I said as Pete sat there in the truck beating his head against the steering wheel. His lips were

Shoot Doggone

moving as he was probably quoting his favorite saying, also.

This time I hooked both log chains together and then to his truck. Within five minutes, Pete's truck was sitting on solid ground. I unhooked the chains and drove to the top of the hill, waiting for Pete. After waiting for five minutes, I drove back down the hill and found Pete stuck again. We hooked the chains up a second time and left them hooked up until we were both safely on top of the hill.

Two minutes after God helped man invent the wheel, the Devil invented a way to get a wheel stuck. Since then, it's been up to mankind to devise ways of getting un-stuck. Throughout history, mankind has dealt with those two common words, *I'm stuck*.

Recently, Joan a very good friend of many years, told us about a time when my dad used those two words. Dad had driven his pickup through our pasture and attempted to cross the creek when he got stuck. After walking a mile back to the house, he told mom, "I'm stuck and I need your help."

Mom was scared to death of tractors. She had grown up in the era of mules. Dad finally convinced her to ride with him on the tractor down to the creek. Dad hooked a chain from the tractor to the truck. He then showed Mom how to drive the tractor with explicit directions on how to let the clutch up very slowly. He would honk the horn when the truck was free from the mud. Dad got in the truck while Mom sat on the tractor.

Mom tried her best but her foot slipped off the clutch causing the tractor to lunge forward and the chain to break. She was so nervous, she kept driving until she got to the house, never looking back!

I'm sure Dad said, "Dag-nab-it!" He probably yelled it as he knew Mom wouldn't hear him anyway! Dad knew it wouldn't do any good to walk home so he walked two miles the opposite direction to our neighbor's house for help.

Lyle, also one of our best friends, chose getting stuck as his hobby. When he got caught up with his farm work, or was bored, he would just take a tractor or a truck and get stuck. He wasn't satisfied getting stuck when the weather was nice and dry. No, he had to do it when it was pouring down rain or drifting snow in sub-zero weather. One of his few free times he took his wife, Joan, for a ride in the pickup truck back in the pasture. Of course, he got stuck. To avoid unleashing his favorite saying, which may or may not be printable, he popped a eucalyptus cough drop in his mouth. These were his favorite and seemed to clear his senses and cool his temper. Lyle and Joan walked back to the house, got the tractor, and drove back to the truck. And you guessed it – he got the tractor stuck. Popping another eucalyptus cough drop into his mouth, he walked back to the house alone. Returning with his second tractor, he was unsuccessful, also – another eucalyptus cough drop. Before the day was over, a neighbor's 4-wheel drive tractor with a long cable had to be used to pull Lyle's trio of mud-covered equipment out. That evening, Lyle made a trip to town to replenish his supply of cough drops.

Another time, Lyle was at the far end of a field when he got his tractor stuck. It was almost dark, so as he walked to the house sucking on his cough drop, he decided to wait until morning to free his tractor. The next morning, he found that the ground had frozen solid around the rear tires. He drove back to his house in the truck sucking on another eucalyptus and got his double bitted ax. Lyle used to tell me the only things he had to play with while growing up was a pony and a double bitted ax, and he had to use the ax to chop firewood.

Over the years, Lyle must have lost some of his ability to swing an ax. While trying to chop the frozen mud away from the big tractor tire, he chopped a hole right into it! Lyle was out of cough drops so the yelling of his favorite saying could be heard all the way across the field.

After that experience, Lyle switched to a new hobby of collecting farm toys. His first hobby had placed him on the verge of eucalyptus cough drop addiction!

Back to my current situation, I didn't mind the walk back to our house. Heavy rains were in the forecast but the clouds didn't look ominous. I was halfway between Pete's house and mine when the clouds opened up, literally drenching me. For ten minutes I walked in a constant downpour, my shoes squishing with every step. As I finally stepped on our porch, a pickup drove by on the same road I'd been walking on for 20 minutes and the rain stopped completely.

My wife met me at the door. "Do we have any eucalyptus cough drops," I asked?

"No, we don't."

"Shoot, doggone!"

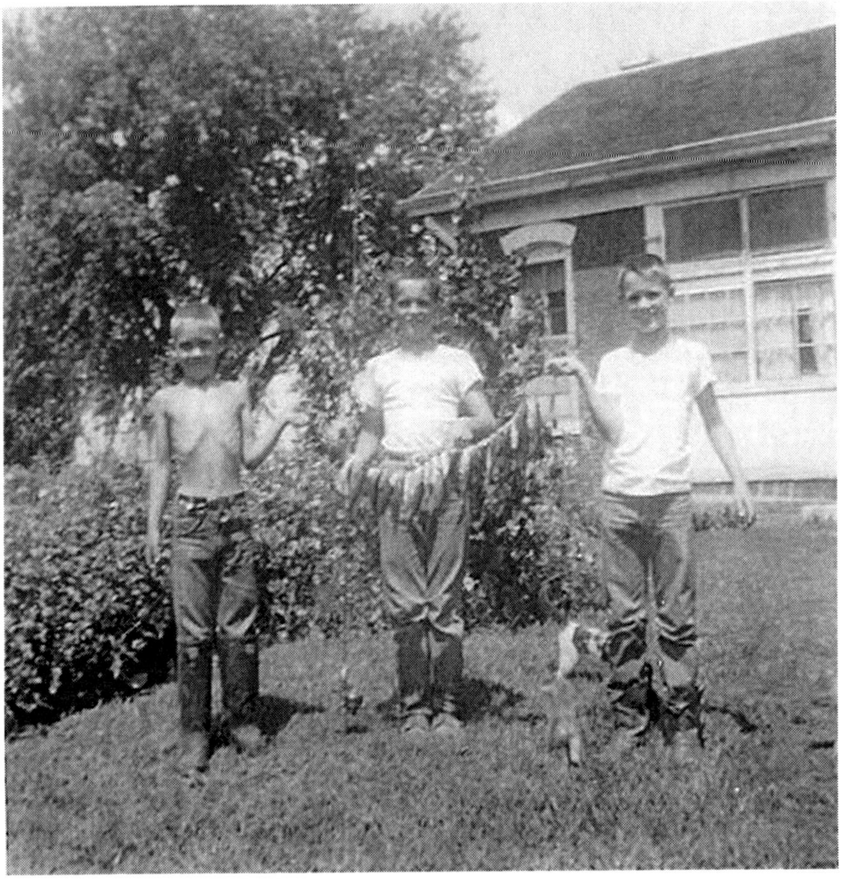

CHAPTER 19

Scat

My two cousins and I were so excited, we could hardly contain ourselves. Lawrence and Leonard, who lived in a nearby city, were spending some of their summer vacation with our family on the farm. Dad and their dad, Uncle Lloyd, were going to take us fishing on McKee Creek. To three boys under ten years of age, who loved to fish, going on a safari wouldn't have excited us more. We dug plenty of earthworms while Dad and Uncle Lloyd gathered the cane poles and fishing tackle which they placed in the bed of Dad's '56 Ford pickup.

It was late afternoon when we arrived at Wilson Ford. Wilson Ford is a shallow area on McKee Creek where you can actually drive across the creek. There was a good fishing hole close to the crossing with a big sandy area. The sandy beach was large enough to keep three boys occupied when they got bored with fishing. We didn't catch many fish but we had a great time playing in the shallow water and looking for fossils.

At sundown, Dad yelled, "All aboard, it's time to head

home." When the three of us started to climb into the cab, Dad really surprised us by asking if we would like to ride home in the back of the truck. We were out of the cab in a flash and Uncle Lloyd helped us climb over the tailgate. What a way to end a great afternoon by being allowed to ride in the back of the truck!

It was approximately fifteen miles from Wilson Ford to our house, so darkness enveloped us before we were halfway home. As the daylight faded, so did our bravery. We began sliding a little closer together for reassurance. Suddenly, Dad slammed on the brakes, bringing the truck to a stop in the loose gravel. He opened his door, jumped out, picked up handfuls of rocks, and threw them toward the darkness at the edge of the road. The three of us boys were terrified as Dad was yelling, "Scat! Get out of here!!"

Dad then jumped back into the truck and took off like he was in a drag race. Lawrence, Leonard, and I kept watching over the tailgate expecting some monstrous cat to emerge from the dust clouds trying to attack us. Thankfully, we made it home safely, but we didn't let any moss grow under our feet as we raced to the safety of our house.

At the supper table, Lawrence was the one with enough courage to ask Dad what he had seen.

"It was a wampus cat," Dad replied. "They are the meanest cats in the world."

We didn't have a clue what a wampus cat was, so I had to be the one to bite the hook. "Well, why are they so mean?" I asked.

Finally, Dad cracked a mischievous grin and replied,

"Because they have a head at both ends of their bodies and they can't go to the bathroom."

Maybe the wampus cat episode was the reason Leonard had another nervous reaction, much later in life, involving big cats.

In the early '80's, there were several rumors circulating that a mountain lion had been spotted in the Kellerville and Siloam State Park area. In the first 3-day deer season, Lyle, Cindy, and I decided to hunt a timber area next to where Lyle farmed just east of Kellerville. Lyle hunted on one side of the farm while Cindy and I hunted in the opposite direction. We were supposed to meet at the truck at noon. Lyle and I each had a walkie-talkie for communication if either of us happened to shoot a deer. After only one hour into our hunt, Lyle's nervous voice came over the walkie-talkie saying, "You guys get back to the truck right away!"

Cindy and I literally ran back to the truck, worried that maybe Lyle was hurt or having a heart attack. Lyle was sitting inside the truck and looked like he had seen a ghost. His face was drained of color and he was chomping on a eucalyptus cough drop.

"Are you all right?" Cindy asked.

"I will be when we get out of here," Lyle replied, "I heard a mountain lion growling!"

Cindy and I knew better than to second guess Lyle's judgment, so the three of us left the area and hunted closer to Timewell.

The following week, on Thanksgiving day, Uncle Lloyd's family arrived to spend the day with extended family. There would be approximately 20 of us to enjoy Mom's and Aunt Esther's great cooking. Previously, I had asked Leonard to bring his archery equipment so we could go deer hunting before the big meal. The thrill of possibly seeing a mountain lion convinced me to take Leonard to the same area where Lyle had heard the cat.

After arriving and parking the truck, I shared with Leonard about Lyle's recent experience. Leonard didn't raise any objections so we made strategic plans for our hunt. I wanted Leonard to have the best chance of shooting a deer, so I instructed him to walk across a large pasture and wait for me at the edge of a timbered area. I would slowly work my way through the timber hopefully driving deer toward Leonard. I watched Leonard, who was over six feet tall, take his long strides across the pasture. I realized he hadn't said a word since I mentioned about Lyle hearing the mountain lion. "Oh well," I thought, "Leonard is as tough as a hedge post. He will stick it out."

After giving him about fifteen minutes to get into position, I began to slowly stalk in his direction through the timber. About ten minutes into the hunt, Mother Nature began knocking on my door. With company at our house, Mom and Cindy had fixed a large breakfast and I suddenly realized I hadn't performed my daily duty before leaving the house. Thank goodness I had some toilet paper in my pocket! Not wanting to risk the dangers of poison ivy, I utilized a wide barren cow path. Feeling much lighter, I continued my drive toward Leonard. The drive was fruitless as Leonard didn't see any deer at all. He seemed relieved when I suggested we head back to the truck. We hadn't taken ten steps when Leonard whispered, "I saw a deer! It went into the timber you just walked through." He suggested that I circle around close to where I started the drive and he would walk through the timber toward me. I'm sure he felt more confident knowing that if I had walked through the timber without being eaten by a large cat, his chances were pretty good, also. I told him there was a good cow path to walk on which would be much quieter than the noisy leaves.

Minutes before I could get to the spot where I wanted to position myself, I could hear limbs cracking in Leonard's direction. Turning to look, I saw Leonard exiting the timber toward the truck, taking strides that would make a gazelle jealous. So much for the hunt!

It was almost an instant replay from the week before. When I got to the truck, Leonard, exactly like Lyle, was sitting inside and his face was drained of any color. When I opened the driver's door, he blurted, "There is a big cat out there! I didn't see him but I saw a big pile where he went to the bathroom and it was still steaming!"

Most people would have burst out laughing at that exact moment and let Leonard off the hook, but I saw a much greater opportunity. Almost choking and holding back tears, I suggested we leave and added that lunch should be ready anyway.

Leonard had stopped shaking and somewhat regained his composure by the time we got home. As soon as we were inside, though, he started talking a mile a minute, sharing with everyone our narrow escape from a man-eating lion. I quickly left the room before risking the danger of hyperventilating. It was after a wonderful meal of roasted turkey and all the fixings, and in front of twenty family members, that I shared "the rest of the story" with Leonard.

Dad and Uncle Loyd seemed to enjoy the humor much more than Leonard. Dad's quick wit emerged as he said, "Well, it couldn't have been a wampus cat.

About the Author

Larry Bullard resides in a rural area close to the small town of Timewell. There is a favorite local saying that, "Time spent in Timewell is time well spent." Most residents, although somewhat partial, will agree with that statement. Many of the memories shared in this book were created in and around Timewell.

This is Larry's first attempt at writing anything more involved than a letter or a note on a Christmas card. Writing a book report in high school English class was a daunting challenge, similar to having a wisdom tooth pulled.

Larry has been involved in farming most of his life. Although retired from the Department of Corrections, he still enjoys the headaches of a small farm utilizing older machinery. He has a variety of interests including deer hunting and making rustic furniture.

Larry is a member of the Timewell Baptist Church. He loves spending time with friends and family, especially his five grandchildren: Devin, Kylie, Hope, Taryn, and Josiah.